The Living Cathedral

Great Bronze Doors at western entrance

The Living Cathedral St. John the Divine

A History and Guide
By Howard E. Quirk

CROSSROAD • NEW YORK

To Barbara, who knows that the
Cathedral is my paramour, yet
loves us both just the same.

Western facade
A. Hansen

1993

The Crossroad Publishing Company
370 Lexington Avenue, New York, NY 10017

Printed in the United States of America

Art Direction/Design by G. Augustine Lynas, NYC

Library of Congress Cataloging-in-Publication Data
Quirk, Howard E.
The living cathedral : St. John the Divine : a history and guide /
Howard E. Quirk
p.   cm.
ISBN 0-8245-1227-8 — ISBN 0-8245-1237-5 (pbk.)
1. Cathedral of St. John the Divine (New York, N.Y.)—History.
2. Cathedral of St. John the Divine (New York, N.Y.)—Guidebooks.
I. Title.
NA5235.N6Q57 1993
726'.6'097471—dc20   93-18660

Contents

Eastern clerestory viewed from ambulatory

Preface

There is a built-in problem with cathedrals, particularly with American cathedrals, and most especially with an American Gothic cathedral on the scale of St. John the Divine. Beyond being impressed and even deeply moved with the size and the awesome beauty, too many visitors whisper, "What is this church actually used for?"

Technically, a cathedral needs little more than room for the bishop's chair (his *cathedra*) and an altar. It could be no bigger than a small chapel; and many of the world's most ancient cathedrals are very modest buildings indeed. In fact, for the first thousand years of Christendom, cathedrals were not usually large churches. For with the sack of Rome and the end of the Roman empire, the classical urban culture of the West and its monumental architectural tradition had sunk into near oblivion. Surrounded by forests and fields, the civilized world was reduced to remote castles and monasteries or an occasional decentralized court. But with the revival of the trade routes across Europe at the end of the twelfth century, market towns once more began to dot the landscape; and soon thereafter the great urban cathedrals of Europe started to rise in such fast-growing cities as Cologne, Paris, and York. The new Gothic cathedrals became immense magnetic institutions of great power and prestige, let alone of physical size. They were the symbolic and often the literal *center* of these new urban areas, signs of a new force at work in the world.

Worship, learning, and commerce all found their expression around the cathedral; and if rain threatened to spoil a market day on the cathedral square, the whole affair might move inside beneath the great arches — potsellers, sheep, and all. The new cathedral was God's house of compassion, spawning hospitals, orphanages, and almshouses, and also became the wellspring of education, art, and science. Perhaps the most respected school of the early Middle Ages was at Chartres; and today's Sorbonne in Paris is a descendant of the cathedral school established at Notre Dame. Theater and music flourished both in the liturgy and on the steps of the cathedral, while shields of the old feudal lords and the new merchant guilds faced each other in the stained-glass windows of nave and transept.

The medieval cathedral was earthy and exalted at the same time. It was big enough to fit the entire city populace inside; and it saw its purpose to be the celebration in God's name of all of the day-to-day life that surrounded it, extending in time and space to include the whole redeemed cosmos as *Corpus Christi*, the Body of Christ.

This background, I hope, reveals something of the modern misunderstanding about cathedrals, especially Gothic cathedrals. The High Middle Ages simply did not separate church and state, or town and gown, or sacred and secular. Also, to complicate matters more, we must remember that many of America's early settlers came to this country precisely *to escape* the pervasive influence of latter-day state churches, whether the Established Church of England or the Roman Catholic or Reformed or Orthodox churches of the Continent. Apart from the Spanish missions of the Southwest and California, America's religious roots just don't contain many cathedral memories. How then shall we make sense of this immense Gothic cathedral in the midst of New York, modern America's most cosmopolitan city?

Because Gothic cathedrals *really do* make sense today! The truth is that we live once more in a *new world* that has seen the earth from the moon for the first time! Just as the new architectural form of the rose window symbolized a change of mind for the Middle Ages, so that photograph of the mysterious blue-green earth wrapped in clouds marks a mind-shift for us. The picture of the earth from the moon has become our new icon, our age's new rose window.

Once again, like medieval people did, we experience unity, wholeness, interconnectedness. With our new ability to explore both the micro- and the macrocosmos, we understand this togetherness afresh. And if we moderns were to design a completely new religious institution for the twenty-first century,

I suspect that it would have something of the feel of a cathedral simply because our understanding of *interconnectedness* and our sympathy for the *livingness* of all creation is what great cathedrals are all about.

At this turn of the century, we face a major local and a major global challenge. Urban poverty runs uncontrolled in New York, in Bombay, in Cairo, all over the world. Also, everywhere the environment in which we all live is rapidly deteriorating. We will solve these twin crises, I believe, only if we make them into very personal involvements, indeed the *contexts* for our faith itself. Like medieval cathedral people, our day-to-day life must become the meat and potatoes of our religion.

Cathedrals by their very nature were created to represent the whole world. They are microcosms, built to enflesh a vision of the Heavenly City right here on Planet Earth. The harmony of interconnectedness that we call Peace (or Shalom or Salaam or Mir) is meant to be visible before our eyes here in busy, complicated New York's Cathedral of St. John the Divine.

For those of us who are about to embark on the twenty-first century, then, perhaps the cathedral contains this secret vision that can help us. In effect, we are already all one people now; all tribes, ethnicities, and nationalities are intermixed cheek-by-jowl. The potential for disharmony is enormous. Indeed, many believe that it is inevitable. But perhaps the cathedral is the unique institution that can give us a vision of that unity which transcends and encompasses our cacophonous diversity — local and tangible, and at the same time global and transcendent.

Could New York's Cathedral of St. John the Divine contain hidden in its vast insides something truly useful and perhaps even saving to us earthlings at the end of our second millennium? No one understands the key to this vision — or can help you to find it in the stained glass, the vaults, the stone, the faces — better than Howard Quirk.

As leader of his own sought-after "Vertical Tour" of the Cathedral for many years, Quirk, himself an ordained clergyman, has led week by week his pilgrims from the bowels of the place into the stratosphere. He knows every nook and every legend, whether earthy or ethereal. Furthermore, as head for twenty years of the Victoria Foundation, he has a long and intimate acquaintance with the global viewpoint that is now being born everywhere and is enshrined at St. John's. The writing of this guidebook is his birthday present

Archangel Gabriel statue atop eastern end   Cathedral Archives

to the Cathedral as we celebrate our hundredth anniversary on St. John's Day, December 27, 1992.

So follow Howard. And if you get lost, remember: the high altar is on the side of the rising sun. ✠

The Very Reverend James Parks Morton
Dean of the Cathedral

Introduction

As Christianity moves toward its third millennium, the church continues to wrestle with the basic challenge it has faced since the early fourth century: balancing upreach and outreach. When Emperor Constantine outlawed persecutions and permitted observance of Christian worship, the church became free to interact and exchange influences with secular society. Opportunity and peril thereafter confronted the faithful.

The greatest peril, of course, lies at the extremes. If the church identifies unequivocally with a political or economic system, it may thrive temporarily but at the cost of selling its soul and reason for being. However, to insulate itself totally from mammon and the profane world is to forsake the Lord's mission and example. A mummified church is a contradiction in terms.

Hence churches and denominations through the ages have sought to travel the golden mean between a pious isolation and a sell-out to secularism. Sometimes the pathway has seemed no broader than a tightrope. It takes a great effort to love sinners while hating sin. Being "in the world but not of the world" is an elusive goal. Still, the commandment "Go forth into all the world..." remains. Not just the nonintimidating world of little children or the innocent world of heathens, but the worlds of art, communication, commerce, law, medicine, ecology, and politics.

Perhaps no fellowship reaches upward with more grandeur and outward with more compassionate zeal than the one at 112th Street and Amsterdam Avenue in New York City. It refuses to tilt toward either piety or humanitarianism at the expense of the other. Nor will it choose between old art forms and new, or ancient and modern liturgical expression. Faced with such "either...or" decisions, the great Cathedral Church of St. John the Divine echoes with the affirmation, "Both!"

The Cathedral's efforts to be all-embracing evoke occasional criticism. But that overarching inclusiveness is actually the best of medieval tradition applied to modern times. Surely it is at the very core of the Cathedral's witness and momentum. In a fragmented society in which our work, our play, our worship, our volunteer service, and our enjoyment of the arts normally take place at different locations with different clusters of colleagues, the Cathedral is a unifying presence. It serves as a hub for all those skewed and disconnected lines radiating from each of us.

The most conservative Christians will discover their dearest symbols and beliefs evidenced in the statuary, iconography, and liturgy at St. John the Divine. Yet the most liberal will find their minds stretched by the Cathedral's range of worship, art, artifacts, and community service.

What other church houses the homeless, provides food and clothing for the needy, counsels those with AIDS, and trains its unemployed neighbors to become builders?

What other religious edifice displays such wonders of God's creation as a huge constellation of quartz crystals, an ostrich egg, and a one-hundred-million-year-old fossil (large-chambered nautilus)?

What other pulpit has been occupied by the Dalai Lama, the mayor of Jerusalem (Teddy Kolleck), the governor of New York (Mario Cuomo), the president of Czechoslovakia (Vaclav Havel), Jesse Jackson, Kurt Vonnegut, and a stream of environmentalists including Barry Commoner, David Brower, Amory Lovins, and Maurice Strong?

What other church, Christian or otherwise, contains Shinto vases, Siamese prayer chests, and Jewish menorah, or portrays in its stained glass Hippocrates, Homer, philosopher Immanuel Kant, and Ottoman jurist Abu Hanifan?

What other fellowship or institution has been so consistently and fervently committed to the survival and health of the planet as to gain assistance from such world citizens as Margaret Mead, Harry Belafonte, Buckminster Fuller, Robert Redford, Buffy St. Marie, E. F. Schumacher, Lewis Thomas, and Carl Sagan?

For each celebrity there are hundreds more of us who find upreach and outreach intersecting magnificently at this huge, hybrid house of God. My own path to this Gotham Gothic church was somewhat circuitous. Born in Women's Hospital at its original location on 110th Street, I was raised in a suburban community church, later trained at a Congregational seminary, and spent most of my working life as the director of a philanthropic foundation. Hence I grew up in total ignorance of chasubles, graduals, and suffragan bishops. Lambeth was nothing more than a rhythmic sidestep. I loved the simple democratic Pilgrim fellowship in which I was brought up; and I still do.

Apparently, however, there was a void in my soul, a yearning for timelessness in architecture and music as well as pageantry in worship. Hence, more than five decades after being carried from Women's Hospital, I found my way back to the vast inner space two blocks away. It was the awesome upreach that attracted me; but the outreach is what held me there. The dozens of programs for the surrounding community and for the planet at large validate this enormous, costly structure in a depressed portion of a beleaguered city.

Since 1980 I have been one of the Cathedral's volunteer guides, a learning, sharing experience that thrusts one into the worlds of art and architecture, Scripture, church history, tradition, and lore plus the many secular professions and events presented in the windows and sculpture. In fact, as the following pages will surely hint, a thorough knowledge of all the people and happenings depicted in stone, stained glass, wood, metal, and tapestries would be the equivalent of a formal education in liberal arts.

This book is intended for those who wish to reduce their ignorance of cathedrals in a hurry. Stated more positively, I have sought to provide a brief summary or frame of reference for major themes presented in the "fabric" of St. John's. Thus, in addition to identifying specific features in some detail, generic paragraphs are offered as background. The short essay on rose windows provides a synopsis of that glorious feature of the Gothic design. The set piece on "religious life" should aid the layperson's appreciation of the window with St. Benedict and St. Francis.

A list of those who have been helpful in the development of this book would be lengthy, even with those inevitable omissions of inadvertence. It will not be attempted. However, duty and gratitude require a heartfelt acknowledgement of my substantial dependency on two compilations that preceded this one. The classic "Gray Book," long out of print, was first published in 1920 by the Laymen's Club and revised sixteen times over the next forty-five years. Dr. Edmund Hagaman Hall was the original compiler and the renowned Canon Edward Nason West a major revisor.

More recent, and still very much in print, is the popular presentation by Canon George W. Wickersham II. Dr. Wickersham's long and intimate association with the Cathedral, coupled with the ability to project his buoyant personality through the written word, have enabled him to be a teacher/friend to hundreds of thousands who never met him in person. To hail his good advice and unflagging encouragement is not meant to inculpate him in any of the deficiencies of this newest effort.

Finally, there is the Cathedral's dean, the Very Reverend James Parks Morton, always larger than life and sometimes better. When I offered to prepare this booklet as a contribution to the Cathedral Church, he said warmly, "One would have to be a bit crazy to take this on, and I think you will do a good job." I was flattered, since the same could be said of the many extraordinary projects — some successful, some not — that have issued from his energies and creative genius. Despite a dizzying schedule that would qualify him as a Christian dervish — religious services, hospital visits, numerous public appearances, incessant fundraising demands, extensive writings, and flights to international conclaves throughout the globe — the dean has regularly found spare hours to improve these pages and to patiently educate this Nonconformist author.

On a small scale, the challenge of this book is like that of the Cathedral itself: to be as broad as possible without becoming shallow. The ultimate achievement would be to shed as much light on the Cathedral Church of St. John the Divine as it sheds on our shared experience of life under God. ✠

Howard E. Quirk
Frost Valley
Claryville, N.Y.

Background

Column ornamentation by Cathedral Stoneworks

Mary Bloom

Choir, sanctuary, and high altar

A. L. Gustafson

[12]

The Origin and Nature of Cathedrals

We often put the question to visiting school groups: "What is the difference between cathedrals and other churches?" "Cathedrals are bigger," is the most common reply from youth as they stare open-mouthed into millions of cubic feet of inner space.

"Usually, but not always," we respond. "It's like men and boys. Men are usually bigger, but not always. There are some little men and some big boys. It's the same with cathedrals and other churches. Size is not the technical difference."

The precise difference is that every cathedral must have a special seat — called a *cathedra* in Greek — in which the bishop of the local diocese sits when participating in a religious service.

This raises further questions. What is a bishop? A church leader whose authority, it is believed, has been passed down from the original church leaders, the Apostles. The outward symbol of this transmission of power comes with the laying on of hands by other bishops in services of ordination and consecration. This establishes a physical continuity extending back to St. Peter, the first bishop of Rome. The Apostolic Succession, as this practice and belief are called, is found in Roman Catholic, Anglican/Episcopal, Orthodox, and Swedish Lutheran churches — those denominations with dioceses.

And what is a diocese? A geographic area including a cluster of churches of the same denomination. The boundaries are not static; they change as populations and the number of communicants (church members) change.

Because of its melting pot nature, New York has more cathedrals (18) than any other city in the world. And for the same basic reason, the United States leads the world in number with 285. Italy follows with 246, most of them small and virtually all of them Roman Catholic. However, the largest church in Italy (and in the world, for that matter) is not a cathedral. This is St. Peter's Basilica in the Vatican.

To explain what a basilica is, we must look back to the early years of the Christian faith. For the first three centuries Christendom had no buildings set aside for worship. Most of the adherents of the new faith were poor and could not afford a separate building. Furthermore, they were under persecution and had to meet in secret. To build a structure would have invited immediate arrest and probable martyrdom. It is true that some of the New Testament writings (the Epistles of St. Paul and the Revelation of St. John the Divine) mention churches. But "church" in those instances referred to a fellowship or group of believers, not a meeting house. More than once St. Paul made reference to "the church which is in their house"; and that is how it was for several generations. Christians gathered in private homes and in secret.

Meanwhile, dating from the Golden Age of Greece, there had been large rectangular buildings, both public and private, called "basilicas." These structures had elevated platforms at the eastern end with a chair of authority (cathedra) for the owner or presider. In a public basilica, it might be occupied by a judge, surrounded by his magistrates. Private basilicas were chaired by wealthy merchants or landowners who might be accompanied by their superintendents at important meetings.

When Emperor Constantine, in the early fourth century, put an end to the persecution of Christians and permitted them to worship "on the first day of the week," their ranks swelled beyond the capacity of private residences. In Rome, the prosperous Laterani family gave its private basilica to the church fellowship; and inevitably its leader (the bishop) occupied the seat of authority (the cathedra) and was surrounded by his priests. St. John Lateran, as the former basilica came to be known, was not only the

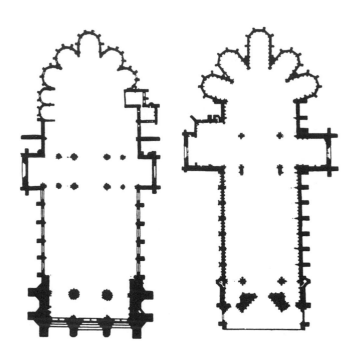

Typical French cathedrals (Troyes and Sees)
with semicircular eastern end

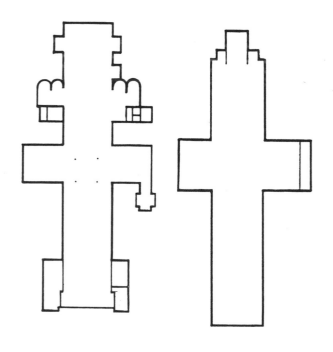

Typical English cathedrals (Winchester and Lincoln)
with squared eastern end

first cathedral; it was, as far as can be determined, the first building set aside and consecrated for Christian worship, the first church structure.

Six other basilicas were given to or built for the Christians of Rome in the fourth century. Latter-day versions of some still survive, notably St. Mary Major and the aforementioned St. Peter's. Throughout the centuries the term "basilica" has been retained to impart special honor to those early houses of worship; and occasionally the pope will award the designation "basilica" to a modern church as a symbol of distinction. But it does not carry the political sense of authority and teaching power that "cathedral" does.

Although more than half of the world's cathedrals are in either the United States or Italy, it is widely agreed that France and Great Britain have the largest number that are venerable masterpieces. When the Gothic style (described under "Rose Windows," pp. 84–87) burst on the scene in France in the twelfth century, it precipitated the greatest wave of church construction in history. A majority of France's ninety-three existing cathedrals date from the late Middle Ages. Only one of them is Protestant, a consequence of an intolerance typified by the persecution or expulsions of the Huguenots. And a majority of them are dedicated to the Blessed Virgin Mary. French cathedrals are marked by a purity of style and a soaring height that is surpassed only in Germany.

The Gothic style quickly crossed the English Channel, where it was often incorporated into existing Norman cathedrals or later adapted to a new form called "Perpendicular." In general, the British cathedrals are the longest of those inherited from medieval times. Their eastern end is usually squared, in contrast with the semicircular apse of the Continent. They lack the purity of those in France but offer a much greater variety. There are sixty-one cathedrals in England alone. The fact that nineteen of them are Roman Catholic is noteworthy, considering that Catholic cathedrals were forbidden from the time of Henry VIII until the mid-nineteenth century. It is also significant that most of Britain's most celebrated cathedrals — Canterbury, Salisbury, Wells, Exeter, York, Ely, Durham, Gloucester — predate the Reformation and were thus built when Rome was the center of power for Western Christianity.

Commentary

The Matter of Size

The Guinness Book of World Records, a perennial best-seller, cites St. John the Divine as the largest cathedral in existence. There is probably a trace of pride in our bearing when we share this fact with visitors. We try, however, to remember that pride is foremost among the seven deadly sins. Nor do we wish to sell out to the secular mind-set, so popular in the Western world, that big is better and biggest is best.

There can be little doubt that some of the world's major houses of worship were inspired more by pride and competitiveness than the desire to glorify God. Such motivation reached its literal zenith when the Protestant Cathedral in Ulm, Germany, built its tower to be one yard higher than that of the Roman Catholic Cathedral (525 feet) in neighboring Cologne. So the first caveat in discussing size is that bigness is a virtue only when it justifies itself and harmonizes with the prayer "Thy kingdom come; Thy will be done."

A second point is that such terms as "big" and "large" are imprecise. Is the biggest person in the world the tallest? the heaviest? the one with the greatest girth? or the one who displaces the most water in the swimming pool? A definition of terms is needed. The same applies to cathedrals. Height, length, width, square feet of floor space, and cubic feet of inner space are all legitimate means of determining size; but the designation of "biggest" depends on which is used.

Finally, the statistics that are available to us have varying degrees of accuracy. Some are rough estimates. Some are reached by multiplying maximum rather than average measurements. Some are rounded off (invariably upward). Occasionally an outdoor piazza seems to have been included as part of the church. The figures given below are from a variety of printed sources considered reliable but not infallible. Unless otherwise indicated, they apply exclusively to cathedrals.

• Internally, the highest, at 155 feet, are Cologne, Germany, and the surviving east end at Beauvais, France.

• The widest, by far, is Seville, Spain at 271 feet.

"Great Sounds for Great Space" concert   Ross Lewis

• Seville also has the greatest square footage of floor space, even if the most conservative figure (128,750) is used.

• At 601 feet, St. John the Divine is the longest cathedral. However, among churches in general it is third, behind the Basilica at Lourdes (656 feet) and St. Peter's Basilica in Rome (611 feet).

• When it is completed, St. John the Divine will also have the most cubic feet of inner space of any cathedral (16,822,000) though it will still be much smaller than St. Peter's Basilica (variously estimated between 30 and 42 million).

• Some of the foregoing statements would be amended if the claims for the concrete-constructed Our Lady of Peace Basilica in Abidjan (Ivory Coast) can be validated. As of 1992, the Vatican had merely denied that it rivals St. Peter's Basilica in size but had neither verified nor refined the publicized measurements.

• Two other cathedrals that were conceived in the twentieth century would also have established new records had they been executed:

In the prosperous 1920s, the Episcopal Diocese of Pennsylvania planned a Gothic church of 640 feet in length. Only the Lady Chapel and two smaller apsidal chapels had taken shape when the Depression put an end to this vision. The chapels and the surrounding acreage were converted to a retirement home in which the ambulatory serves a worthy purpose not originally foreseen.

Larger still was the original design for the Roman Catholic cathedral in Liverpool, England. It called for the following dimensions (St. Peter's are shown in brackets for comparison): length, 680 feet [611]; width, 400 feet [320]; square feet of floor space, 233,000 [163,000]; diameter of dome, 168 feet [137]. As the crypt was being completed, the realities of financing forced a major retrenchment of plans, resulting in a circular (actually sixteen-sided) church built over the center of the crypt. The crypt entrance, a full city block away, is a reminder of the extent of the earlier dream.

CB

What about the matter of size and the size of matter in a House of God? Can a tremendous stone cathedral be justified in present times? Not on purely pragmatic grounds. The upper 90 percent has no utilitarian function; a ten-foot ceiling could easily accommodate the tallest human beings. Moreover, any furnace heat in winter travels quickly to that unused area above.

A great cathedral can be justified only by its meaning and its impact. It glorifies God only as it speaks to God's children. Size is but a means to an end. Were size an end in itself, the Astrodome and the Superdome, each several times larger than any cathedral, would be shrines. Their meaning, however, is evanescent and terrestrial; it speaks not to the great issues of our existence.

In a later chapter, "Outreach" (pp. 151–152), those commitments and services that comprise the heart and life blood of St. John's service to the community are described.

Wood carving on choir stall   Cathedral Archives

Size is not a guarantor of holiness. Inherently, a cathedral is no more sacred than the humblest Quaker meeting house. And our Quaker Friends would tell us that their worship centers are no more sacred than a home or a place of work or a field or a street. They would remind us that it is the light within that is sacred. Doubtless true. But there are many of us for whom the scalp tingle and the heart leap produced by a great cathedral church ignites and rekindles that light. The awesome space, with its ancient symbols and its reminder of Emmanuel (God with us), weans us away from pettiness, banality, and self-absorption and points us again toward the New Jerusalem envisioned by St. John the Divine.

The sense of awe, the worship of God, and the service to humankind comprise a cardiovascular system that justifies its immense anatomy.

The Revelation of St. John

There is no other first name as commonly used in the Western world as "John," when all the variations are included (Johann, Ian, Giovanni, Juan, Ivan, Evan, Jean, etc.). More than sixty of the saints bear that name; so it is inevitable that there will be confusion at times. Not that John the Baptist is ever confused with anyone else, so singular were his words, diet, and dress. Still that leaves John the Apostle, John the Evangelist, John the author of three short New Testament Epistles, and John the Divine.

Were they all the same person? That belief has been held in various quarters since the second century and remains popular among conservative Christians. Many scholars, however, believe that there were at least two and possibly three or four men filling these roles. The question is intriguing but not in any sense crucial to the faith. We can simply give thanks for the great Johannine contribution to Christianity whether the source is single or manifold. The patron of our Cathedral is St. John the Divine; and "Divine" in this instance, is a noun, not an adjective. The translation "St. John, the Theologian" is just as accurate and probably more helpful, for that is the meaning of "Divine" in this setting.

The Revelation of St. John was destined to be the concluding book of the Holy Bible. Not only was it among the last to be written; it is also a summary, from a Christian perspective, of the Judaeo-Christian odyssey that emerges in the preceding biblical books. And finally it is a vision beyond this earthly age to the New Jerusalem in heaven.

Some seminaries devote a semester class to this extraordinary apocalyptic writing. A guide book such as this can offer only the briefest glimpse of St. John's monumental work. A full appreciation and understanding of Revelation requires a careful reading and a reasonable familiarity with the Scripture that precedes it plus the assistance of a scholarly commentary that explains the setting, symbolism, vernacular, and objectives of this biblical benediction.

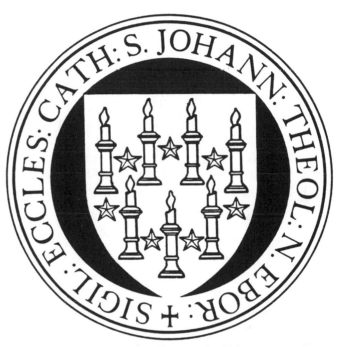

The seal of St. John the Divine

St. John wrote at the turn of the first century as an exile on the island of Patmos. The era was one of intense persecution, and the writer seemed to have two audiences in mind. In an immediate sense there were seven churches in nearby Asia Minor, each already showing singular strengths, weaknesses, and needs — some of which the author mentions. The bulk of his words, however, appear to be addressed to a broader readership: Christians throughout the Roman empire and for generations yet to come, Christians who need spiritual support in times of severe trial. The use of a letter as a vehicle he adopted from St. Paul; but the content of the Revelation is more reminiscent of grim Old Testament prophecies, especially the visions of Daniel and Ezekiel.

The climactic vision of the New Jerusalem and the proclamation of God's triumph, Christ's reign, and the deliverance of the faithful constitute a unique and powerful conclusion to the book and to the entire Christian canon.

[17]

Ever since the advent of the Gothic style of architecture in the twelfth century, with loftier vaulting and large stained-glass windows providing new dimensions of beauty, cathedrals have been designed to represent the New Jerusalem of St. John's Revelation. The inspired use of marble, tile, and glass in soaring churches illuminated by color-filtered sunlight has not only strengthened the faith of believers but has spoken to the souls of visitors in ways that no other tourist stop could do. As Winston Churchill has observed, "We fashion our buildings and then they fashion us."

It is unlikely that any church would incorporate all of the symbolic and numerological references in the final book of the Bible, but use of the number seven has been the mark of many cathedrals. St. John's vision included seven seals, seven bowls, seven candles, seven trumpets, seven stars, seven churches. In this he was following a tradition already venerable: seven days of creation, seven required forgivenesses, seven ears of corn in Pharaoh's dream, etc. And long afterward the Middle Ages were to add to the septology by delineating seven sacraments, seven deadly sins, seven cardinal virtues, and seven joys of Mary, as well as the Stations of the Cross (which are double seven).

In our Cathedral dedicated to the author of the Revelation, the architects and iconographers were ever mindful of those writings. The Lesser Rose Window is divided into seven sections, each containing depictions of St. John's vision. There are seven bays on each side of the nave, seven apsidal chapels, seven stars and seven candles in the Cathedral's coat of arms and seven clerestory windows in the ambulatory.

ಚಿ

Does the Revelation speak to the age of science? Major external enemies in our time include environmental deterioration, substance abuse, hunger, homelessness, and crime. Most of these problems are in some way related to internal flaws, harmful priorities held by God's children. And since it was inner space that Christ came to conquer, his message — set forth in the Gospels, codified in the Epistles, and crowned by the Revelation of St. John the Divine — remains eminently and ultimately relevant.

Jewish and Christian symbols at high altar   A. Hansen

The History of the Cathedral's Construction

The construction of this cathedral building can be likened to a symphony. There is a long overture followed by two contrasting movements, an intermission, and then an ongoing final movement. Schubert's Unfinished Symphony is apt to be the prototype for many decades to come.

The Overture (1828–92)

A clandestine meeting took place between a political leader and a prelate. Shades of the Borgias or Cardinal Richelieu or Henry VIII. But this was in Manhattan in 1828. Bishop John Henry Hobart, head of the Episcopal diocese, was consulting with New York City's mayor, Philip Hone.

The question at hand: Would it be feasible to build an Episcopal cathedral in New York? There were no church structures in America to match the great cathedrals of Western Europe. Why not erect one in the gateway city of our new nation?

Mayor Hone, himself an Episcopalian, was sympathetic but wary. As a direct derivative of the Church of England, the Episcopal Church was regarded as a Tory institution by many who could remember the Revolutionary War and the more recent War of 1812. Moreover, the Dutch, whose ancestors had settled the city as New Amsterdam, were still a presence and a power. An Anglican cathedral would not be popular with them either. "Where is the money," asked the mayor, "where the public spirit, where the liberality to carry such a noble plan into execution?"

Political wisdom, which sometimes serves God better than piety, prevailed, and it was not until after our nation's most deadly war that the question was again raised, this time by a layman. At the behest of Stephen P. Nash, a New York attorney representing the sentiments of several churchmen, Bishop Hor-atio Potter brought the matter before the diocese at its 1872 convention. Remarkably, there was unanimous approval to move ahead; and the New York State Legislature expeditiously granted a charter the following April.

Nearly two decades elapsed between the necessary approvals to build and the actual laying of the cornerstone. The main cause of this protracted delay was the financial panic of 1873, the consequences of which were felt throughout the business and nonprofit worlds for a dozen years. Institutions were hard-pressed to keep basic commitments and survive; and virtually no construction was undertaken. In the case of the Cathedral there was also the matter of finding the best building site, choosing an architect, and selecting a plan.

The four gigantic arches of the crossing

Crossing and eastern end (from 110th St.)

Bishop Horatio Potter died in 1887 and was succeeded by his nephew, Henry Codman Potter, who brought youth and zeal to the cathedral project. Our nation was experiencing an unprecedented wave of immigration, most of it through the Port of New York, and this inspired diocesan leaders to envision their future cathedral as "a house of prayer for all nations." The seven "Chapels of Tongues," which eventually curved around the eastern end of the Cathedral, were dedicated to the major groups of European immigrants of that time. The location in New York of the United Nations in 1946 underscored the foresightedness of this concept; and the Cathedral has enjoyed a close, supportive relationship with UN leaders since that body was established.

The Romanesque Movement (1892–1911)

The contest for the design of the new Cathedral had produced nearly one hundred entrants and a great variety of architectural styles ranging from the conservatively traditional to unrestrained fantasy. Among the proposals that were turned down were two from Ralph Adams Cram, a man in his midtwenties. The award was given to the New York firm of Heins and LaFarge, whose design called for a composite Romanesque/Byzantine/Gothic structure.

The architectural competition had been preceded by the search for a proper location. The heart of the city had moved steadily northward during the nineteenth century; and in anticipation of a continuation of that trend, a thirteen-acre parcel at the southeast rim of Morningside Heights was finally chosen. George Macculoch Miller, an active layman, is credited with calling this tract to the attention of Bishop Potter.

The site, largely wooded, was owned by the Leake and Watts Orphan Asylum, an institution in financial need. A price of $850,000 was set, a daunting amount at the time. However, Bishop Potter managed to raise it from families within the diocese. Thus the asylum was able to move to a less expensive site in Yonkers and enjoy a substantial endowment. None of the Cathedral leaders could possibly have foreseen the variety of important uses to which the old orphanage building would be put during the century following its purchase (see "The Cathedral Close," pp. 147–150). When the south transept is constructed, this original building, erected in the 1820s in the Federal style, will probably be relocated within the Cathedral's precinct and continue to be a functional part of the close.

Miller later became president of St. Luke's Hospital and was instrumental in moving it to the tract directly north of the Cathedral. Shortly thereafter Columbia University, of which George Macculoch Miller was also a trustee, purchased its acreage to the immediate north and west. Suddenly Morningside Heights became a slightly self-conscious acropolis with Anglican-rooted institutions for body, mind, and spirit rising from its bedrock.

That bedrock, it was soon discovered, did not spread evenly through the area. Excavation for the Cathedral, begun soon after the cornerstone laying on December 27, 1892 (St. John's Day), yielded loose rock, compressible earth and underground springs. Only the faith of the bishop and J. P. Morgan, plus $500,000 from the latter "to get us out of the hole," kept discouragement from prevailing at the sight of the huge pond that filled the excavation while the entire structure of St. Luke's Hospital was being built across the street.

The first, or "Romanesque," phase of construction saw the completion of the choir area (including presbytery and high altar area) and two of the apsidal chapels (see the chapters "The Apse and Ambulatory," pp. 97–99, "The Choir, Sanctuary, and

The nave taking shape   Cathedral Archives

Presbytery," pp. 127–129, for definitions). In place as well were the four gigantic granite arches forming the crossing. The arches were sealed on three sides with temporary concrete walls but open to the choir.

Also intended to be temporary was the dome over the crossing. Like the vaulting throughout the Cathedral, as well as the vaulting of the crypt and undercroft area, the dome was made of light but solid Guastavino tiles. Over a thousand other American structures feature such tiles; but this Cathedral had the personal, day-to-day attention of the Rafael Guastavinos, father and son. During the ensuing years the dome has won such fame and admiration that it may be preserved on that faraway day when the western towers and the transepts are completed and final attention is turned to the central tower.

Assembling a nave rosette   Cathedral Archives

Western facade in process (from 112th St.)   Cathedral Archives

Although Bishop Henry Codman Potter was truly the leader and driving force during the first phase of construction, his task was considerably eased by the assistance of the Reverend William Reed Huntington, beloved rector of Grace Church, whose chairmanship of the Fabric Committee virtually overlapped this period. His was the voice of calm and compromise when clergy and wealthy laity disagreed on various aspects of the new, unprecedented structure.

The Gothic Movement (1911–41)

Three of the dominant players in the first movement died within months of each other: George L. Heins, of Heins and LaFarge (1907); Bishop Potter (1908); and Dr. Huntington (1909). The Cathedral's contract with Heins and LaFarge had stipulated that

the death of either partner of that firm would permit a termination of the agreement.

Meantime, the Gothic style, which had been regarded with outright disdain for over three centuries, was coming back into favor, influenced by the long-delayed completion of Germany's Cologne Cathedral in 1882. In Boston, Ralph Adams Cram, whose immature plans had been rejected two decades earlier, now emerged as the foremost neo-Gothicist of the era. Cram and his colleagues Frank Ferguson and Bertram Goodhue were responsible for the Chapel at West Point, Princeton University Chapel, St. Thomas's on Fifth Avenue, and more than a hundred other American churches.

The leaderless building project, the wave of neo-Gothicism, and the availability of Cram enabled those who had championed a Gothic structure from the outset to prevail at long last. This time Cram did not have the luxury of starting from scratch; his chance for self-indulgence was greatly circum-

The nave nearly completed

Schoonhals

scribed. He was expected to take a half-built structure (already larger than a majority of the world's cathedrals) and redeem it, improve it, and complete it (see "The Nave," pp. 41–42 for details of this challenge).

From pencil sketches in the archives, it appears that Cram, a brilliant perfectionist, was his own harshest critic. More than any Cathedral trustee, he could spot inconsistencies — esthetic and symbolic — in proposed plans. Years later, in reflecting on his career, he acknowledged that the original Heins and LaFarge plan had been superior to his own. He also asserted that the finest of all the early proposals had come from Bishop Potter's brother, but was turned down to obviate any charges of nepotism.

The nave foundation was laid in 1916; but World War I and the shortage of funds delayed further progress at the western end. Gifts from wealthy families, however, permitted the building of the five remaining Chapels of the Tongues at the eastern end. Only one of these (St. Martin of Tours Chapel) was designed by the Cram firm.

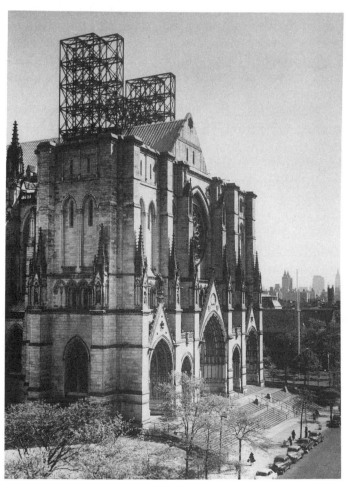

Skyscrapers begin to appear in the south   Cathedral Archives

Henry Codman Potter had been succeeded by Bishops David Greer and Charles Burch, both of whom were supportive of the building project. But the next forward surge in construction awaited the consecration of the Right Reverend William Thomas Manning in 1920. Bishop Manning became to the nave of St. John's what Abbot Suger had been to St. Denis Abbey, Maurice de Sully to Notre Dame, Paris, and Edward the Confessor to Westminster Abbey: promoter, advocate, impresario, and champion. The bishop was charismatic before that word had become narrowly co-opted. Excerpts from Canon Wickersham's book capture the whirlwind resulting from this prelate's contagious zeal:

"There was a surge of fervor for the whole undertaking. Emotions ran high. School children, societies, churches, poor people, rich people — all gave to help build 'Big John.'

"The scope of the drive was, in retrospect, breathtaking. There was an all-star track-meet in Yankee Stadium. Vince Richards played Bill Tilden on the championship court at the Forest Hills Tennis Club. The world's leading polo players vied at Meadowbrook. George M. Cohan, Al Jolson, Julia Marlowe, Otis Skinner, Ann Harding, Blanche Yurka, Lillian Braithwaite, Crystal Herne, and E. H. Sothern — luminaries extraordinary — appeared together on the stage of Hampden's Theatre. Nothing was too much for the Cathedral. In charge of all this was a busy young lawyer named Franklin Delano Roosevelt.

"Few questioned the validity of the undertaking. A model of the completed cathedral stood in the north balcony of Grand Central Station, the object of daily scrutiny by thousands of commuters and travelers — a symbol of civic pride. Even the 'Great Depression' of 1929–36 did little to dampen the mood. On the contrary, the employment of so many laborers, artisans and artists was viewed as a highly commendable measure."

As the nave neared completion, it became obvious to interested parties that when the temporary wall between nave and crossing was removed, it would unite two sizeable church structures of differing and clashing architectural styles. To give esthetic integrity to the entire space, Cram was authorized to replace the vaulting over the LaFarge choir and the eastern portion of the apse. Worship during that three-year labor was moved to the nave, with portions of the pipe organ placed on the north and south sides of the provisional sanctuary.

The nave was dedicated on November 30, 1941, in a service spangled with the noble ecclesiastical theater that the Anglican-Episcopal tradition plans and executes so superbly. In addition to the nave, a unique and awesome space, the public was now seeing the full interior — the greatest indoor length (601 feet) of any cathedral in existence. "Two football fields, end-to-end, with room left for the football" became the popular imagery for comprehending more than a ninth of a mile of uninterrupted view. It was also noted that the Washington Monument, laid on its side, would fit comfortably into the Cathedral with enough additional space for a tennis court at the western end.

The Intermission (1941–72)

Once again, a conflux of unanticipated events brought to an end a phase of the Cathedral's construction. Foremost was the bombing of Pearl Harbor, which took place exactly a week after the nave dedication. Ralph Adams Cram died the following year and Bishop Manning retired shortly after World War II. Moreover, the increasing decay and poverty of neighboring Harlem cried out for attention and assistance. In such circumstances it seemed immoral to add the embellishment of towers to a church building that was already functional. Construction ceased and would not resume for four decades.

The Open-ended Finale (1973–　)

In the early 1970s a new leadership team came in the persons of the Right Reverend Paul Moore, thirteenth bishop of New York, and his hand-picked dean, the Very Reverend James Parks Morton, seventh dean. Both men brought strong credentials as supporters of civil rights and social reform. Therefore, when Dean Morton raised the prospect of resuming construction of the Cathedral, the primary questions were practical rather than moral. New York City had barely moved back from the brink of bankruptcy. Was this the time for such a quixotic venture? Shouldn't the Cathedral stick with its human services commitments in this period of mounting unemployment and poverty? The dean had a thoughtful response, which started with an echo of Matthew 26:11:

"If all construction in history had awaited the eradication of poverty, nothing would ever have been built. Furthermore, the stonework will be done by our own unemployed and underemployed neighbors. We will revive the art of stonecraft and eventually complete the world's largest cathedral. And we will provide our city with a massive symbol of hope and rebirth."

These words, and the supporting commitment of the Cathedral's trustees, were courageous and inspiring. The concept was profoundly and ineffably romantic. A cathedral growing above Harlem, like the tree growing in Brooklyn, captured public imagination. But the task was monumental both figuratively and literally.

Stonecraft at all levels (building, cutting, carving, and setting) was a moribund skill in the United States. Professionals had to be brought from England to create a stoneyard and convert unskilled trainees into journeymen stoneworkers. Then there were trade unions to be dealt with and the prospect of increased rates for trainees but fewer of them. With the backing of Harlem leaders, the Cathedral elected to forego union affiliation and grant its own journeymen's certificates in the medieval tradition. A shortage of funds, one of the most universal besetments for nonprofit endeavors, was a constant concern.

Nonetheless, the stoneyard was dedicated on June 21, 1979; and on September 29, 1982 (the feast of St. Michael), the first stone was laid in the southwest tower during an unforgettable ceremony in which aerialist Philippe Petit walked across a high wire 150 feet above Amsterdam Avenue to deliver a silver trowel to Bishop Moore. One cynical reporter suggested that under existing conditions this was safer than crossing at street level; but the overwhelming reaction of the media and the city was one of enthusiasm and hope. This highly dramatic event symbolized much of what the Cathedral seeks to do in New York: to be an integral part of its existence and revival and to aid its residents in the celebration and commemoration of life.

And the construction program? The seemingly quixotic dream of the 1970s has matured into an eminently practical operation in which the human dimension remains unchanged, but the tools of the trade include instruments unprecedented in the history of stonework. Digital cameras, robotic saws and routers, and a linear motion table reduce the monotony of repetitive work and greatly accelerate production. Meanwhile, a separate profit-making, tax-paying entity, the Cathedral Stoneworks, was incorporated in 1989 with a mandate that goes beyond the continuing construction of the world's largest Gothic church building.

Stone cutters whose progress was slow-paced and confined to elemental work in earlier years can now program machines to do much of the fabrication needed in capitals, friezes, entablatures, and reliefs, and do it at a relatively swift pace. Construction and restoration becomes more accurate and economical as twenty-first-century technology is applied to the thirteenth-century goal that started this program.

As a consequence, the Cathedral Stoneworks is available for outside work. The first contracts included the Carnegie Mellon College of Fine Art in Pittsburgh, the Jewish Museum and the Coca Cola Building in Manhattan, and a number of churches. This is a boon for the metropolis that contains more stone structures than any other on the planet. Thus do the completion of the Cathedral and the rebuilding of the city proceed hand in hand in a new Stone Age.

When will the building be complete? Friendly wagers are sometimes placed with full confidence that the bettors will not be around to pay off or collect. And most of them are not disturbed by that reality. There is something deeply dynamic about a cathedral in process. Its incompleteness matches that of humankind. Like an unfinished crossword or jigsaw puzzle, it commands our attention and involvement in a way that the completed puzzle cannot do. The yearning to build on earth the New Jerusalem, which was envisioned by the theologian St. John the Divine, imparts momentum and gives direction to all who share it, even though it cannot be fulfilled.

Cutters and carvers in stoneyard crew

Robert F. Rodriguez

 *Commentary*

A Citywide Church

There are thousands of churches in New York City. Each worships God and answers human needs or it would cease to be a church. But few have the commitment and none the space to be as all-embracing as Big John. Memorial services for a wide range of citizens have been held here — from Duke Ellington to puppeteer Jim Hensen; from Eleanor Roosevelt to John Belushi. New York's school chancellor, Dr. Richard Green, was not an Episcopalian but his request that his memorial service be held at Big John was honored by his family, who also appreciated the space and spirit of this church. Nor was the celebrated choreographer Alvin Ailey of the Anglican tradition; but his troop held its memorial dance in the vast Gothic space on Amsterdam Avenue. Leonard Bernstein was not Christian; but he had been a Cathedral Colleague for years. The dean and chapter gratefully acknowledged his contributions to Christian music and world music by hosting the concert of remembrance for him.

There is unity in joy as well as sorrow. The election of Vaclav Havel as president of Czechoslovakia shortly after his release from prison triggered a cathedral extravaganza of welcome. Zubin Mehta, Plácido Domingo, Dizzy Gillespie, Henry Kissinger, Paul Newman, Roberta Flack, Elie Wiesel, James Taylor, Arthur Miller, and Joseph Papp were among those who spoke or performed in a candlelight service of thanksgiving with President and Mrs. Havel.

A great portion of the Cathedral's witness does not involve celebrities or casts of thousands. The recycling program engages a faithful handful; the counseling programs for those with AIDS or their survivors are one-to-one relationships, as are the letters to prison inmates. The hand-painted cross with scenes of bloodshed from Somoza's Nicaragua speaks to some; the menorahs near the high altar speak to some; the Shinto vases have special meaning for others. Thus does the Cathedral testify to the belief that God is the circle whose center is everywhere and whose circumference is nowhere. Rabbi Kelman of the Conservative Rabbinical Assembly said, "The remarkable thing about the Cathedral is that it is equally comfortable for the homeless and the celebrity."

Bishops of New York

First:	Samuel Provoost (1742–1815): bishop of New York (1787–1815).
Second:	Benjamin Moore (1748–1816): assistant bishop (1801–15); bishop of New York (1815–16).
Third:	John Henry Hobart (1775–1830): assistant bishop (1811–16); bishop of New York (1816–30).
Fourth:	Benjamin Treadwell Onderdonk (1791–1861): bishop of New York (active, 1830–45; inactive, 1845–61).
Fifth:	Jonathan Mayhew Wainwright (1792–1854): provisional bishop of New York (1852–54).
Sixth:	Horatio Potter (1802–87): provisional bishop (1854–61); bishop of New York (1861–87).
Seventh:	Henry Codman Potter (1834–1908): assistant bishop (1883–87); bishop of New York (1887–1908).
Eighth:	David Hummell Greer (1844–1919): bishop coadjutor (1904–8); bishop of New York (1908–19).
Ninth:	Charles Sumner Burch (1855–1920): suffragan bishop (1911–19); bishop of New York (1919–20).
Tenth:	William Thomas Manning (1866–1949): bishop of New York (1921–46).
Eleventh:	Charles K. Gilbert (1878–1958): suffragan bishop (1930–47); bishop of New York (1947–1950).
Twelfth:	Horace William Baden Donegan (1900–1991): suffragan bishop (1947–50); bishop coadjutor (1950); bishop of New York (1950–72).
Thirteenth:	Paul Moore, Jr. (1919–): bishop coadjutor (1969–72); bishop of New York (1972–89).
Fourteenth:	Richard Frank Grein (1934–): bishop of Kansas (1980–88); bishop coadjutor of New York (1988–89); bishop of New York (1989–).

Deans of the Cathedral Church

William Mercer Grosvenor 1911–16
Howard Chandler Robbins 1917–29
Milo Hudson Gates 1930–39
James Pernette DeWolfe 1940–42
James Albert Pike 1952–58
John Vernon Butler 1960–66
James Parks Morton 1972–

Exterior

St. Peter statue–Trumeau, north tower porch
Cathedral Archives

Statue of St. John and newer sculpture on central porch

[28]

The View from Outside

Unless one is born in a cathedral, the initial sight of it is external. And for those who never do enter, that is the only view. The interior may tell the story of the faith in minute detail through exquisite art; but the exterior statement comes first.

What does it say? Spires and fleches are fingers pointed heavenward. Towers, historically, have been seen as bastions of defense against a secular, profane, and sinful world. The cruciform architecture may, for the faithful, evoke that Death which triumphed over death. The great stone buttresses, rising and then springing to a central arch, remind some observers of Albrecht Dürer's "Praying Hands" writ large.

The initial glimpse of a great house of worship is often from afar and occasionally unforgettable. A white spire thrusting above the New England foliage or a mosque shimmering across the desert sand produces a stirring deep within. Sheer size may be part of the impact. Until the last century, the world's tallest enclosed structures were churches. Even today a few of the great medieval cathedrals — Ely, Gloucester, Cologne — dominate their human-made surroundings; and the incomparable asymmetrical spires of Chartres are visible for miles in every direction.

Churches can be photogenic without enjoying sweeping, unobstructed vistas. Notre Dame, Paris, viewed from the left bank of the Seine, offers a classic picture of Gothic strength and beauty. Salisbury, a perpendicular gem set on the green velvet of a 160-acre close, has inspired Constable, Turner, and sundry lesser artists.

A promontory location sometimes provides an advantage to an ancient church as it competes with modern high-rise buildings for a place in the urban silhouette. Lincoln and Durham are so favored in England as is the Cathedral of the Sacred Heart in Newark, N.J. Surely the apotheosis of stunning church settings was achieved long ago in the Abbey of Mont Saint-Michel. Built atop a massive rock jutting out of the Normandy flats, this otherworldly apparition becomes even more chimerical at high tide.

Dramatic though reflecting waters and manicured lawns are in highlighting buildings of worship, they do not speak to one crucial aspect of the view from outside. How does a church relate to the people? How accessible is it to the masses? How relevant to human needs are its offerings? Are there visible signs of outreach?

This is quite different from such features as size, setting, symmetry, and silhouette, but it is central to an institution's profile as a house of God. In sad truth it must be said that some of the most celebrated of Europe's ancient churches have become little more than high-domed museums and tourist stops with worship conducted regularly only for the clerics and a handful of laity. By contrast, there are churches of lesser fame, stature, and antiquity whose service to the downtrodden is the work without which faith is dead.

The sight of the destitute entering the rooms beneath St. Martin's in the Field in London tells the outside observer the church has soul. The good done throughout New York by Trinity Church parish speaks as religiously as the creeds, chants, and sermons heard within the walls of that Victorian edifice. A church is a fellowship before it is a building.

When the first huge crossing arch at the Cathedral of St. John the Divine was erected at the turn of the last century, it could be seen from New Jersey and Queens. Gradually skyscrapers and apartment houses have reduced this visibility to a small section of nearby Manhattan.

As for the closer external appearance, St. John is enhanced or diminished by its incompleteness, depending on one's vantage point. Beheld from the

Western entrance (exit) after Stoneyard dedication 1979

Beverly Hall

southeast, it suggests to the observer that the losing bidders were never notified and all proceeded to build. Amid the vertical clutter of wood, bricks, stone, and concrete can be seen five Doric columns, four chapel gablets, three nine-foot statues, two granite buttresses, and one medieval turret. The absence of a partridge in a pear tree is compensated for by the presence of a peacock and a fig tree in the Biblical Garden at the foot of this architectural potpourri.

The western facade, on the other hand, is vitalized by its incipience. The scaffolding promises that the rising towers will complete the vertical thrust needed to balance the horizontal power of Ralph Adams Cram's geometric triumph.

It is, of course, the statement of this huge building and its usage that justify the thousands of stones and millions of dollars required in construction. It is the combination of upreach and outreach, the love of God and the love of humankind, the feeding of spiritual hunger at the Eucharist and the feeding of physical hunger in the basement below that validate and ennoble the structure.

The view from outside tells much about St. John's inner spirit. Watch the people coming to commemorate the Holocaust or to pray for peace. Note the homeless, many of whom are housed each night. See the dancers, the musicians, the environmentalists who draw spiritual nourishment here. Observe the AIDS victims or their survivors, grateful for a clear sign of acceptance. And then there are the atheists dissatisfied with their void and the agnostics who yearn for a symbol more heroic than a question mark.

Roger Kennedy, former head of the Smithsonian Institution, sums it up: "St. John the Divine is more important for what it does than what it is. The masonry mass performs a symbolic function of calling attention to the long tradition of Christian service to the community."

Master carver Simon Verity working on the Portal of Paradise, central porch

Robert F. Rodriguez

Artist's rendering of completed western facade

The Western Facade

All medieval cathedrals and abbeys and most modern ones are oriented on an east/west axis. The tradition probably originates in sun worship but was incorporated into Christian architecture, where it acquired added symbolism. One enters from the west, leaving behind death, symbolized by the setting sun, and looks east to the altar, behind which is the rising sun representing the risen Son of God.

In many cases, including St. John the Divine, this tradition cannot be followed with compass precision. The existing grid of streets requires an adjustment. For aesthetic purposes, a cathedral needs to be oriented at right angles to the street on which it is built. Since Amsterdam Avenue does not run perfectly north and south, our cathedral could not be built exactly east and west.

Because the western facade includes the main entrance, it is always wider than the nave to which it offers admission. A tone of grandeur is thereby established. At 207 feet in width, St. John's facade is nearly 50 percent broader than its nave. Often the contrast is greater. The facade at Wells, England, is twice the width of the nave. In some instances (such as in Mexico City and Santiago de Compostela, Spain), the wall of an adjacent museum or church is so blended with the cathedral front as to comprise part of a massive religious rampart.

The western towers of a cathedral are almost invariably flush with the remainder of the entrance facade. A notable exception is the Cathedral of the Sacred Heart in Newark, N.J., where the towers have been rotated forty-five degrees forward. A dramatic, three-dimensional entrance is the result. A wider facade is achieved without the need for extra stones; and a feeling of welcome and embrace issues from the fabric of the church to approaching worshipers and visitors.

One of the nostrums of Western architecture is that the exterior of a building should foretell the interior. Just as a faithful book cover will suggest the theme within, so should the inner character of a cathedral be heralded by its facade.

The five western entrances at St. John the Divine Ⓐ, Ⓑ, Ⓒ, Ⓓ, and Ⓔ, framed by the six great piers Ⓕ, announce five aisles within. The horizontal walkway immediately above them Ⓖ matches the nave triforium. The Great Rose Window Ⓗ, flanked by two Gothic windows Ⓘ, Ⓙ, anticipates the clerestory stratum of the interior. A more detailed preview of theme and subject is provided in the sculpture within the porches and the sixty biblical scenes on the Great Bronze Doors. These are identified individually below.

Highly symbolic are the horizontal pedestal lines. The lower one Ⓚ comes at eye level for the average adult standing outside. The next level Ⓛ matches the eye for those who have mounted the six steps into the porches or portals. The same pillar base exists within the nave. The message is clear. Humankind may use itself as the measure of all things; but everything in heaven is higher and lifts human sights and aspirations accordingly.

Most cathedral fronts are asymmetrical. The north tower is not identical to the south. They are like the right and left sides of the human face — imperfectly balanced. The differences may be subtle, the sort of irregularity that we notice in a friend's visage only when we see our friend's reflection in a mirror. Or they may be striking. The cathedrals at Strasbourg, Ulm, and Ely have single western towers with no aesthetic counterbalance. Chartres's asymmetry is less dramatic. Still, the western towers there are of distinctly different heights and styles.

Like a majority of western fronts, St. John's variations are relatively quiet. Notice the horizontal bands on the diagram. The lowest, or portal, section is balanced; the latitude of the Great Rose Window has variations; the Kings Gallery above returns to a left/right mirror image; but each tower has a distinctive character.

Architecturally, St. John's western facade — like the entire structure — shows a distinct French Gothic influence with echoes of an English style. The Great Rose Window is a classic Gothic trademark. The presence of five portals evokes the fronts of Bourges and Wells; but the porch depth is more like that at Amiens or Peterborough.

For decades the horizontal power of our towerless structure dominated 112th Street and vicinity. As the towers reach upward toward completion (St. Paul's on the right or south; St. Peter's to the left or north), they give an equally awesome verticality to the Cathedral's mien. The upreach and the outreach that mark the fellowship within will be majestically symbolized by the finished facade.

Of special interest to senior New Yorkers are the bronze lights on the Cathedral's steps. These once illuminated Pennsylvania Station, a landmark now gone from the scene; they continue to provide a beacon for travelers, albeit of a different variety.

Details *Existing and Planned*

A **North Tower Porch** (p. 32). The statues are the work of John Angel, one of the outstanding sculptors of his time. At the centerpost, or trumeau, is St. Peter, holding the keys to heaven. Beneath his feet is the cock that crowed when he denied his Lord. The basestone shows the disciple before the accusing servant, striking the high priest's servant, and receiving his commission to feed the flock. The figures of eight martyrs flank the valves of the doorway, each with a basestone indicating the form of the martyrdom. **On the north side** left to center:

• St. Thomas Becket/his murder and the subsequent scourging of Henry II. • St. Stephen, the first martyr/his stoning. • St. Catherine of Alexandria/her mystic marriage and her confounding of the doctors. • St. Alban, the first British martyr/shown protecting a missionary.

On the south side, right to center:

• St. Denis, first French martyr and patron of France/ after being beheaded, he carries his head to Montmartre. • St. Joan of Arc/ her vision; her rousing the soldiers to battle; coronation of Charles VII and Joan's martyrdom at the stake. • St. Vincent of Saragossa, Spanish deacon and patron of wine growers/ shown defying the ruler and being buried at sea.

• St. Lawrence of Rome, patron of the poor/his being burned on the grid and his intercession for the soul of the emperor.

At the apex of the porch arch is the Holy Rood: Christ on the Cross with St. Mary and St. John beneath.

B **and** D **North and South Entrances,** through which daily access is gained to the Cathedral. The two sets of doors in each entrance are made of Burmese teakwood.

C **The Central Porch.** Beneath the apex of the arch covering the central porch is a statue of Christ in Glory (called *The Majestas*) surrounded by the seven lamps and seven stars described in Revelation 1:12–16. The entire work, executed by John Angel, comes within a large stone circle that permits daylight to illuminate the Lesser Rose Window (see "Rose Windows," pp. 84–87). The curved triangles on either side (called spandrels) are for the symbols of the four Evangelists (angel, winged lion, winged ox, and eagle). On the centerpost below (trumeau) is St. John gazing upward to *The Majestas* to record his vision (see "The Revelation of St. John," pp. 17–18).

E **The South Tower Porch.** Matching the eight martyrs depicted in the North Tower Porch, the south porch presents stone carvings of eight theologians: St. Francis of Assisi, St. Bernard, St. Boniface, St. John Chrysostom, St. Dominic, St. Gregory, St. Patrick, and St. Athanasius.

M **The Great Bronze Doors,** given in memory of Haley Fiske, were sculpted by Henry Wilson and cast by Barbedienne of Paris, who also cast the Statue of Liberty. They consist of four valves, each of which is eighteen feet high and six feet wide and weighs three tons. The bas relief on the northern set depicts events from the Old Testament. The pair to the south shows New Testament scenes. There are sixty events in all.

N **The Portal of Paradise.** For over half a century, twenty-four massive uncarved stone blocks flanked the Great Bronze Doors of the principal entrance. In September 1988, under the direction of British sculptor Simon Verity, stone carvers developed in the Cathedral's training program began to give shape to thirty-two figures — kings, prophets, judges, farmers, parents, and children of the Jewish faith in which Christianity is rooted. The plan had been set forth by Ralph Adams Cram in 1925. The final sequence and choices were made by the Cathedral dean, James Parks Morton, in consultation with Jewish and Christian clergy (see photo, p. 31).

Martyrs on north side of north tower porch

⊡ **The Kings Gallery.** Connecting the bases of the two great towers are six gables, each with two niches, and two pinnacles with larger niches. This stratum of a cathedral that, with the triforium, divides the entire facade into three horizontal sections is traditionally called the Kings Gallery, dating to a time when the statues of the kings of Israel would occupy the gable niches. Those will not be filled in this cathedral. However, the two pinnacle niches will be occupied by major figures in the Old Testament. A nine-foot statue of Moses ⊡ will fill the niche of the north pinnacle while Elijah ⊡ will look down from the southern pinnacle.

Towers of St. Peter and St. Paul. Rising three hundred feet above the nave floor and an additional hundred feet above the bedrock from which they start will be two of the most formidable western towers in Christendom. The cornerstone for the upper portion of the St. Paul tower ⊡, set in 1982, is "The Jerusalem Stone" inscribed in Hebrew, Arabic, and English, a gift of Jerusalem's mayor, Teddy Kolleck.

St. Paul's tower will hold a carillon (a set of bells that can be played manually from a keyboard or programmed automatically). St. Peter's tower ⊡ on the left, or north, will hold a "peal" of twelve bells, which will be rung in the time-honored style — one ringer per bell — in various patterns and permutations popularized in England. An additional Bourdon bell, larger than the others and named "Great William" in honor of William Thomas Manning, tenth bishop of New York, will toll the hours and mark special occasions. It will also honor another man with the same Christian name, William B. Van Nortwick, donor of all thirteen bells in the Tower of St. Peter.

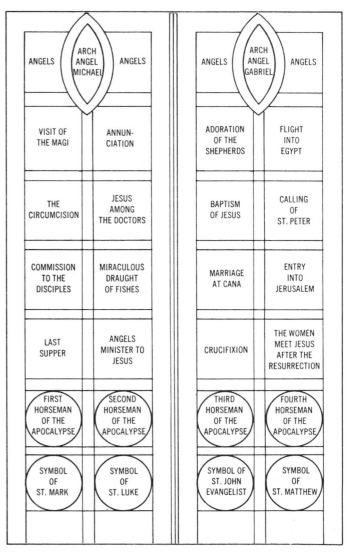

Great Bronze Doors

Western Interior

Liturgical dancers beneath Great Rose Window   Robert Desakay

Western triforium surmounted by state trumpets and Great Rose Window

A. Hensen

The Narthex

There was no defined narthex in Ralph Adams Cram's plans, no enclosure or demarcation between the west end of the Cathedral and the nave. Later, medieval choir stalls, on permanent loan from the Metropolitan Museum of Art, were placed one bay to the east of the towers, creating a narthex (foyer) to separate entering crowds from worshipers. At 180 feet in width and 85 feet in maximum depth, this "vestibule" is as large as many parish churches and is beautified by orthodox icons on the screen that backs the choir stalls.

In addition to the two rose windows that dominate the western end of the Cathedral, there are four sizeable Gothic windows in the narthex/tower area west of the nave. In keeping with the numerology and symbolism of St. John's Revelation, these windows are each comprised of seven medallions: three in each lancet plus a crowning rosette. In traditional style they are each numbered from the bottom starting with the left lancet.

A **The Prototype window** (p. 40), the work of Ernest W. Lakeman, is in the south wall of the south tower. Only the top portion can be seen when the door to that tower is closed. Represented are 1 Sacrifice: Abraham is about to sacrifice his son, Isaac, in the belief that it is God's will (see Gen. 22:1–13) for the full story and the happy ending. 2 Priesthood: Melchizedek (Gen. 14:18) is shown in full pontificals attended by angels. 3 Wisdom: Koheleth, associated with Solomon in ancient Hebrew writings, is portrayed. 4 The Law: Moses has the two stone tablets of the Ten Commandments. 5 The Prophets: Isaiah is dictating to the angel scribe the prophecy which is now so well-known because of Handel's "Messiah." 6 Royalty: King David is seated with scepter and crown. In the rosette at the top 7 Jesus is seated between the two disciples whom he met on the road to Emmaus. Jesus became the fulfillment of preceding prototypes; hence the window title.

This window is a combined memorial: The rosette was given in honor of St. Monica by Miss Caroline Phelps Stokes. The lancets were given by Charlotte A. Hamilton in memory of her father, John C. Hamilton, and mother, Maria Eliza Hamilton.

B Above the south portal is a small window showing the Crusader cross of Peter the Hermit. C Beneath, and continuing the theme of dedicated travel, is a stone frieze showing Canterbury Christians centered on St. Thomas Becket. D The facing frieze on the north wall shows Paul on the Damascus Road.

High above the entrance doors flanking the Great Rose Window are two grisaille windows with a special silvery luminescence popular in medieval times. They were made by Charles J. Connick.

E **The southern grisaille,** a memorial to Emma W. Scott features the seven archangels: 1 St. Michael holds a sword and scales, symbols of power and justice; 2 St. Gabriel holds lilies; 3 St. Uriel has a radiant sun; 4 St. Raphael, a fish; 5 St. Zadkiel, a sacrificial knife; 6 St. Chemuela, a chalice; and 7 St. Jophiel, a sword.

F **The northern grisaille** has symbols of the seven churches of Asia: 1 Ephesus, 2 Smyrna, 3 Pergamos, 4 Thyatira, 5 Sardis, 6 Philadelphia, and 7 Laodicea. This window is the gift of Fannie A. Jackson in memory of her father and mother, Thomas R. Jackson and Charlotte Bailey Myers Jackson, and her sister, Charlotte Louise Jackson.

G Over the north portal is a small window showing the Holy Grail of Joseph of Arimathea. H Beneath is a stone sculpture of Crusaders, and facing I is a sculpture of Jesus washing the feet of St. Peter.

J At the northern end of the north tower is the **Creation window** by Ernest W. Lakeman. 1 Day One: "Let there be light" (Gen. 1:3) is given a Christian perspective with Christ shown as the Light of the World (John 8:12). 2 Day Two: The firmament is divided from the waters of the earth (Gen. 1:6–8); ③ Day Three: The waters and dry land are separated (Gen. 1:10). ④ Day Four: Day and night are separated (Gen. 1:14–15). ⑤ Day Five: The seas produce creatures that swim, walk, and fly (Gen. 1:20); ⑥ Day Six: Man ("Adam" in Hebrew) is created in God's image (Gen. 1:26–27); note the hand of God; ⑦ Day Seven: God rests (Gen. 2:2). In the triangular tracery are ⑧ Judaism, represented by the seven-candle menorah, and ⑨ Christianity, represented by a chalice. The twelve signs of the zodiac can be found in the lancet borders. The window was given by Mrs. E. C. Ludlow in memory of Gabriel Ludlow.

Anyone standing in the center of the narthex and facing west will first note the Great Bronze Doors. These doors are described in detail under "Western Facade" (see p. 34) and are more interesting when viewed from outdoors since the external panels capture great events in the Old and New Testaments. On the inner side there are simply floriated designs and plaques.

Above are the Great and Lesser Rose Windows, described in a separate chapter (pp. 84–87) and best viewed from the eastern end of the Cathedral. Between the windows is a rank of sixty-one state

trumpet pipes, one of the loudest organ stops in existence. They are under control of the organ console more than five hundred feet to the east (see "The Choir, Sanctuary, and Presbytery," pp. 127–31 for further description).

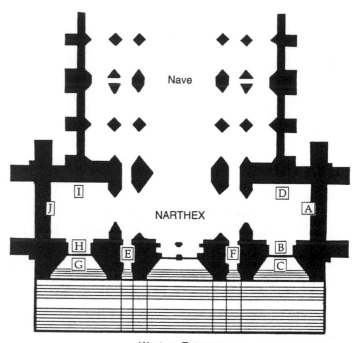

Western Entrance

Prototype Window

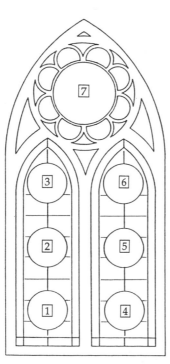

Southern Grisaille Window

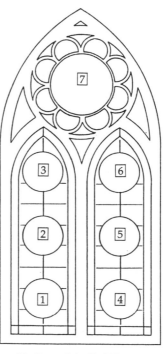

Northern Grisaille Window

Creation Window

The Nave

If Ralph Adams Cram had designed the entire Cathedral, it is very unlikely that his nave would have been as large, as magnificent, or as singular as the one that he was obliged to create. Cram inherited a partially built structure that was already wider and longer than the eastern end of any Gothic church in existence. The width of his nave was dictated by the immense diameter of the crossing; and the length had to equal the combined length of the existing crossing, choir, and easternmost chapel if the completed structure were not to look truncated.

Cram's own retrospective comments were typically insightful: "Our mandate had been to go on in Gothic. . . . This did impose certain limitations but they were just those limiting factors that stimulate and control rather than hamper and confine." Necessity mothered a massive invention comprised of the following unusual features:

• There are three rows of piers on each side of the nave. The outer rows would be external buttresses in a medieval church; but here the interior of the church has been widened to include them.

• Consequently, the flying buttresses, so prominent in the exterior of European churches, fly internally at St. John the Divine and can be seen in the form of bridges and chambers above the side aisles.

• As they proceed east and west, the piers are alternately wide (sixteen feet in diameter) and slender (six feet in diameter). The slender pillars, by edict of the city engineer, are solid, scalloped blocks of granite, weighing four tons each. There are fifty-three courses or layers of them in each slender pillar. The larger pillars have a granite base, above which is a granite interior faced with limestone.

The result at the top is a sex-partite vault in which each pair of inner piers is connected by an arch, but only the massive pillars are connected by diagonal (or groin) ribs. The great nave is thereby divided into a system of four double bays (squares) instead of eight rectangles. This is not unique in the world, but rare.

• Six rows of interior columns produce five aisles, distinguishing St. John's from a majority of Gothic cathedrals. Only the inner three currently serve as passageways; the outer aisles are used for chapels and exhibits.

• The clerestory (topmost) windows of the north and south walls are not flush with the innermost ranks of piers as in all medieval cathedrals (Bristol, England, excepted). They are attached to the middle rows of piers. The upper reaches of the church are thereby widened, the visitors' viewing angle for those windows is improved (better perspective, fewer neck cramps), and the slender innermost pillars rise a hundred feet without attachment before springing to make the vaulted ceiling. Nothing comparable is to be found in any other church in the world.

Although Anglican theology long ago moved away from the concept of the clergy as intermediaries or intercessors for the laity, the identification of the east end of a church with the priests and choristers and the west end, or nave, with the laity remains. Architect Cram took this into account when he made the figure of Jesus in the western rose window the size of a human being in contrast with the red-robed reigning Lord at the east end, six hundred feet away. He also made the pedestals of the inner piers reach to eye height for the average human being.

Most of the fourteen bays of the nave (seven each along the north and south walls) celebrate contributions made by various lay groups within society: artists, athletes, lawyers, communicators, doctors, soldiers, government leaders (American History Bay), social workers (All Souls' Bay), and laborers.

Matters that are spiritual in significance but not particularly priestly in nature are often addressed in the nave in an ever-evolving series of exhibits. Bishop Manning set the tone when he moved a city tenement into the west end of the nave. Half a century later there was a salt marsh beneath one of the arcade windows and an AIDS memorial in an adjoining bay. In such instances there is always the hope, on the part of the dean and chapter, that improved scientific discovery and maturing human values will render the displays obsolete.

Topical banners pleading for the release of hostages or the cessation of armed support to foreign nations are often exhibited for extended periods; and a thirty-five-foot Christmas tree, decorated with a thousand white paper cranes of peace, has often graced the narthex during Advent season.

The columned arcade above the bays is the *triforium*, which provides an east-west walkway on each side of the nave. On the interior sides of these walkways are open spaces between pillars; against the outer walls are windowless rooms. These offices and spaces are made available to a variety of people who are contributing to the various artistic, humanitarian, and spiritual thrusts of the Cathedral fellowship. The work of a prominent writer, a world-renowned aerialist, and an interfaith agency are examples of the activities going on in a portion of the building that in most cathedrals has become as useless as the human appendix.

Above the triforium is **the clerestory** level with huge windows (forty-five feet in height), which usually highlight the theme of the corresponding bay windows far below. There are sixteen of these uppermost windows, one above each of the fourteen bays plus one over each of the two entrances at the eastern end of the nave. Atop the clerestory level are stone ribs springing inward to form the Gothic arches crowning one of the most remarkable naves extant. The distance from the floor to the apex of these arches is 124 feet, a height exceeded in only a few cathedral naves (Cologne, Ulm, Amiens, and Palma).

Separating the nave from the eastern half of the church is the massive **Children's Arch** built in the mid-1920s with funds contributed by school children of the City of New York and gifts made in memory of children. Worshipers partaking of the Eucharist pass beneath this arch to reach the altar evoking the Scripture passage, "Unless you become like little children, you will not enter the kingdom of heaven."

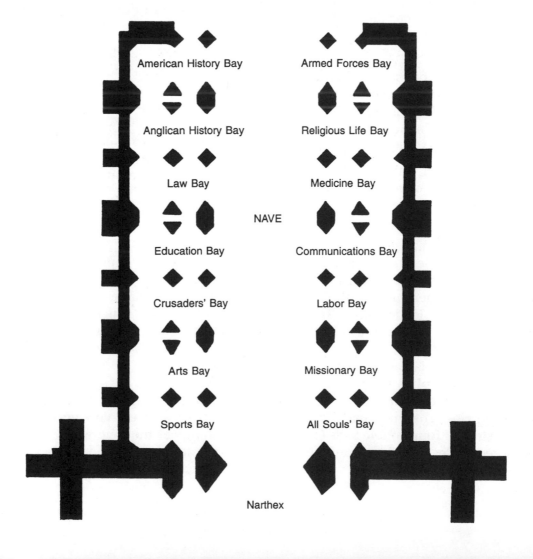

American History Bay

Armed Forces Bay

Anglican History Bay

Religious Life Bay

Law Bay

Medicine Bay

NAVE

Education Bay

Communications Bay

Crusaders' Bay

Labor Bay

Arts Bay

Missionary Bay

Sports Bay

All Souls' Bay

Narthex

The Sports Bay

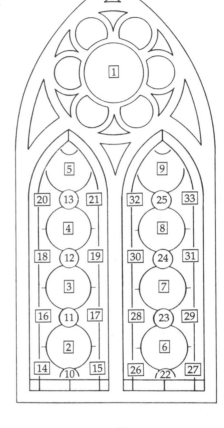

Within the Sports Bay (first on the north) is one of six nave chapels. The frontal on the altar, consisting of reindeer hide and beading, was made and presented by Alaskan Indians in memory of Bishop Rowe and Archdeacon Stuck.

1 The bay is dedicated to St. Hubert (656–728), who somehow inherited the legend of the second-century martyr St. Eustache: While hunting, he encountered a white stag whose antlers formed a gleaming crucifix. This ended his hunting career and converted him to the Christian faith, where he rose to the position of bishop at Liege. Ironically, Hubert has become the patron of hunters while also one of the saints of animal protection.

One of two dozen sports depicted in window   Gregory Thorp

Major medallions: 2 Esau the hunter (Gen. 25:27); 3 Jacob wrestling with the angel (Gen. 32:24); 4 David conquering Goliath (1 Sam. 17:49); 5 St. Paul's injunction to run the good race (1 Cor. 9:24); 6 Elijah and the chariot (2 Kings 2:9–15); 7 Samson killing the lion (Judges 14:5–6); 8 St. Matthias chosen by lot to take the place of Judas, who had committed suicide (Acts 1:23–26); 9 St. Paul's injunction to put on the whole armor of God (Eph. 6:11).

Minor medallions: 10 Bowling; 11 Auto racing; 12 Swimming; 13 Figure skating; **Side-niches:** 14 and 15 Boxing; 16 Ice Hockey; 17 Football; 18 Baseball; 19 Basketball; 20 Tennis; 21 Fencing.

Minor medallions: 22 Sculling; 23 Tobogganing; 24 Sailing; 25 Bicycling; **Side niches:** 26 and 27 Archery; 28 Hunting; 29 Soccer; 30 Skiing; 31 Polo; 32 Fishing; 33 Golf.

 *Commentary*

Good Sports

"What's basketball and skiing got to do with a church?" asked a school boy as he studied the figures in the stained-glass window. Fortunately, others had raised the same question earlier, so the tour guide was ready for him. "If something is worth doing, it should be done in a way that pleases God. Right? If it isn't worth doing, you don't do it at all. Sports are a legitimate and noble part of our common life, as long as we participate in an honest, fair manner. All worthwhile activities are part of God's world and should be of concern to the church."

Still, it *is* unusual to have a twenty-five-foot stained-glass window (taller than a two-story house) portraying archery, boxing, tennis, and other sports.

Correspondence from the mid-1920s (when the iconography of the nave windows was being planned) offers insight into some of the social and moral values of that era. Billiards, swordsmanship, and pistol practice, marginal in the minds of some church leaders, were, in fact, limited to tiny symbols in the margins of the window. The suggestion of depicting trap shooting was effectively shot down by a thoughtful appeal from the Audubon Society.

It is not surprising that polo was originally granted a commanding position in the window. Cathedral supporters included many of the super-rich. Conversely, basketball, an infant sport, was to have been tucked away in a corner. This evoked protest from a perceptive clergyman in Pittsburgh. He wrote, "It is hard for those of us in touch with the present situation in the sporting world to see why polo should be classified as a major sport and basketball relegated to a position among minor sports.... I venture to say that for one person interested in polo, there are a thousand devoted to basketball.... In our Parish Church we have five basketball teams. It is hard to imagine any church which could afford to support a polo team."

Sports are defined as physical recreation. But the very experience of re-creation is largely attitudinal. It is a restoring change from the burden of bread-winning toil. Fishing is not a sport for the Eskimos. Baseball, basketball, and football are big business for many professional athletes, their agents, and their players' unions. Such complexities could not be ad-

dressed in stained glass. Nor did they trouble the Right Reverend William T. Manning, who presided over and inspired all aspects of completing the Cathedral nave. Bishop Manning repeatedly affirmed, "Our play and our work have as real a place in our lives as our prayers."

As a human being, Bishop Manning was truly a "good sport" as he sought to put his church in touch with all walks of life, confident that the benefits would flow both ways. The archives reveal a man in perpetual motion: organizing a swimming meet at the Brooklyn "Y"; arranging for a huge track meet at Yankee Stadium (general admission, fifty cents) and serving as one of the time-keepers; "planting" an editorial endorsement in the *New York Times;* persuading a socialite to head the Golf Committee. And quite apart from sports, there were thirteen other topical windows in the nave for which he was also making plans and raising funds. Meanwhile, his tasks as shepherd of a growing diocese proceeded apace.

A fascinated observer said, "That man sure kicks up a lot of dust." And when the dust had settled, there was a unique Sports Window, thirty-seven other nave windows, and forty-six piers and buttresses to show for the effort. The bishop's own dust is entombed five bays to the east; but his real monument is the entire nave, which in itself is larger than most of the world's cathedrals.

Biblical and modern figures in Sports Bay window   Gregory Thorp

The Arts Bay

The Arts Bay was given by Lillian Sefton Thomas Dodge in memory of Vincent Benjamin Thomas. The Shakespeare stone on the right side of the bay came from a sedilia canopy in a chapel of the parish church of Stratford-on-Avon, England. Like the clerestory window above, the Arts Bay window was made by Charles J. Connick.

[1] **The rosette** in the window shows St. Dunstan (908–88), Benedictine monk and reformer, who became archbishop of Canterbury. During his days as a hermit in Glastonbury, he learned the crafts of painting, embroidery, and metalwork and has become the patron of artists, craftsmen, and bells. He is shown repulsing the temptation of the devil with the tongs from his forge.

Arts and crafts fill **the six cusps,** or petals, of the surrounding circle: [2] stone-carving, [3] manuscript illumination, [4] embroidery, [5] stained-glass work, [6] metal work, and [7] wood-working. The triangular tracery shows [8] a harp; and [9] bells symbolizing the music of praise.

The center ovals in the left lancet read from bottom to top: [10] Architecture: David instructs Solomon in planning the Temple (968 B.C.E.); [11] Sculpture: Michelangelo (1475–1564) carves his heroic figure of David; [12] Poetry: The mystic rose of Dante (1265–1321) is shown with small figures of the Virgin Mary and St. Bernard. [13] Music: Choristers sing from atop Magdalen Tower, Oxford, in the annual May Day celebration.

The border depictions of the left lancet are read left to right from the bottom: [14] Iktinos (fifth century B.C.E.), architect of the Parthenon; [15] Christopher Wren (1632–1723), architect of St. Paul's Cathedral, London; [16] Phidias, from the golden age of Greek sculpture (fifth century B.C.E.), with a model of the Parthenon; [17] Donatello (1386–1466), first major Renaissance sculptor, with his figure of St. John the Baptist; [18] Homer (tenth century B.C.E.), father of epic poetry (*The Iliad* and *The Odyssey*); [19] Shakespeare (1564–1616), father of English drama; [20] Murbecke, sixteenth-century musician who composed the first music for English liturgy; [21] Palestrina (1526–94), composer of hymns and masses, considered the father of harmonic music.

The center ovals in the right lancet read from the bottom up: [22] Early Christian Architecture: Emperor Justinian (527–65) and his architects plan the great church of Hagia Sophia (Holy Wisdom) at Constantinople; [23] Painting: *The Majestas*, by

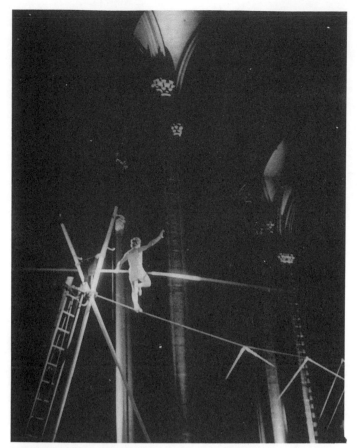
Cathedral artist in residence Philippe Petit crosses the nave

Muppeteers at Jim Henson memorial service

The Nishikawa Troupe Japanese dance theater

The Dance Theater of Harlem
Cathedral arts events

Ralph Lee's production of "Wild Man"

Mary Bloom

[46]

Duccio (1255–1319) is carried through the streets of Siena in festival procession; [24] Engraving: Albrecht Dürer (1471–1528), whose *Apocalypse* is a noble example of this art; [25] Gothic Architecture: The octagonal lantern with which Alan of Walsingham brilliantly replaced the fallen tower at Ely Cathedral, England, is suggested by turrets.

The border depictions of the right lancet read left to right from the bottom: [26] Giotto (1276–1337), architect and painter who is regarded as the father of modern art; [27] Fra Angelico (1387–1455), devout painter-monk; [28] Abbot Suger (1170–1245), shown with a model of the abbey at St. Denis, which launched the building style now called "Gothic"; [29] Augustus Pugin (1812–52), credited with starting the Gothic revival of the nineteenth century; [30] Rembrandt (1609–69), Dutch painter and interpreter of Gospel subjects; [31] Berruguete (sixteenth century), Spanish sculptor and painter; a student of Michelangelo; [32] William of Wykeham (fourteenth century), first exponent of the Perpendicular adaptation of Gothic architecture, found primarily in England; [33] Brunelleschi (1377–1446), whose daring engineering for the dome of the cathedral in Florence helped launch the Italian Renaissance.

cs

The Poets' Corner

In the year 1400, a respected clerk and diplomat, whose house abutted Westminster Abbey, died and was entombed in that great church. Years later, when his literary talent was more fully recognized, Geoffrey Chaucer became regarded as the first of many to be honored in the Abbey's Poets' Corner. During the ensuing centuries many people of letters have been entombed or marked in that setting: Thackeray and Dickens, Spenser and Goldsmith, Jonson and Johnson, Wordsworth and Southey, Eliot (George) and Eliot (T. S.). A lively game of literary hopscotch can be enjoyed if the vergers aren't looking.

Inspired by this tradition, our Cathedral has established its own Poets' Corner, memorializing such American men and women of letters as Emily Dickinson, Mark Twain, Washington Irving, and Edgar Allan Poe. Unveiled in 1984 by the late Marie Bullock, honorary chair of the Poets' Corner, in a ceremony highlighted by the participation of Walter Cronkite, Gregory Peck, and Robert Penn Warren, the Corner consists of black slate floorstones engraved with the names, dates, and brief identifying phrases of outstanding native poets and novelists. Each year two new names are chosen by the Cathedral's poet electors under the direction of the poet in residence.

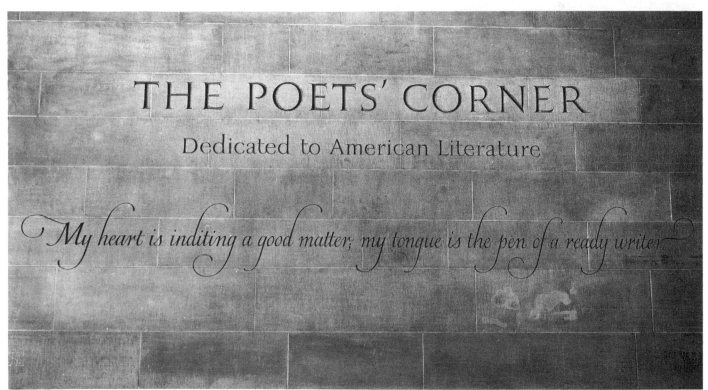

Wall of Arts Bay

Robert F. Rodriguez

The Crusaders' Bay

The third bay on the left (north) aisle as one proceeds toward the altar is dedicated to Crusaders. As indicated in the following essay, the Crusades were a complex and sometimes ignominious chapter in Christian history. The Cathedral's iconographers have presented the topic in a thoughtful, positive way. **The rosette** at the top of the window Ⓐ sets the theme. It shows the Heavenly City envisioned by St. John, a reminder that our true and ongoing Crusade is to work toward the dominance of Christ's spirit in our lives and world.

The bay was given in memory of D. Willis James by his son, Arthur Curtiss James. The window was made by Ernest W. Lakeman.

Left Lancet

Major medallions: ① Jerusalem captured by the Turks in 1070; ② Council of Clermont, 1095; ③ Peter the Hermit preaching the First Crusade; ④ Godfrey de Bouillon taking the Cross.

Subordinate medallions: ⑤ Pope Urban II appointing Adehemar leader of the First Crusade; ⑥ followers of Raymond of St. Gilles flocking to his standard; ⑦ Godfrey pledging his land to the bishop of Liege; ⑧ Tancred taking an oath in service of Emperor Alexius; ⑨ Pope Urban giving the banner of St. Peter to Hugh the Great; ⑩ Emperor Frederick II at the treaty signed by Sultan Kameel.

Right Lancet

Major medallions: ⑪ armies setting forth; ⑫ misfortunes of the Crusader; ⑬ Crusaders capturing Jerusalem; ⑭ Godfrey de Bouillon made king.

Subordinate medallions: ⑮ Eleanor of Acquitaine holding court in Antioch; ⑯ Baldwin of Flanders crowned Latin emperor of the East; ⑰ Emperor Frederick II entering Jerusalem; ⑱ St. Bernard preaching the Crusade to Emperor Conrad II; ⑲ Pope Innocent III instigating the Fifth Crusade; ⑳ St. Louis leading the Eighth Crusade.

The quarter circles at the bottom level honor the works of latter-day crusaders against human oppression and disease: ㉑ John Milton (1608–74), blind English poet, writer, and early crusader for freedom of the press; ㉒ William Wilberforce (1759–1833), English politician and philanthropist; earliest leader to oppose slavery; ㉓ Walter Reed (1851–1902), American bacteriologist and army officer who made advances against yellow fever; ㉔ Hideyo Noguchi (1876–1928), Japanese bacteriologist whose research at the Rockefeller Institute helped identify and control venereal diseases.

 *Commentary*

Cross and Crescent

In the autumn of 1095 Pope Urban II addressed the leaders of the Western church (more than six hundred bishops and abbots) at the Council of Clermont. His sermon, a clarion call to free Jerusalem from the barbarous Turks, had far-reaching consequences. For the next two hundred years that message competed in spirit with his Lord's Sermon on the Mount.

There is no other instance in history of such a prolonged pageant of chivalry and shame, innocence and treachery, genuine devotion and corrupted zealotry as was seen on the byways of Europe and in the cities at the eastern end of the Mediterranean in the twelfth and thirteenth centuries. The popular term of enlistment became "taking up the Cross," hence "crusade" from the Spanish word *cruzada*.

The extremes of human character, revealed in conflict and hardship, pitting against each other two of the world's most aggressive religions, were the stuff of theater. Thus have they been well exploited and frequently romanticized by observers from Raymond of Aguilers down to modern-day script writers. Irresistible is a cast that includes:

• Peter the Hermit, a medieval John the Baptist, a crude holy man who recognized and seized a cause that seemed transcendent.

• Stephen of Cloyes, a French shepherd boy whose vision and charisma launched the quixotic and disastrous Children's Crusade.

• The three kings from the Occident who spearheaded the Third Crusade: Philip II of France, Frederick Barbarossa (Red Beard) of Germany and Richard II (Lionhearted) of England.

• Saladin, incomparable Saracen leader whose name would be enshrined in song had not all of the minstrels been on the opposite side.

• Richard the Lionhearted, whose gallantry and occasional successes in battle captured the fancy of the troubadours, Robin Hood, and history.

• Eleanor of Acquitaine, brilliant and powerful wife of two kings (Louis VII of France and Henry II of England) and mother of two kings (Richard II and John). Eleanor instituted the courts of love in which the plaints of the heartsick were judged. She is thereby credited with elevating the status of women and enhancing the age of chivalry.

• Louis IX of France, who emerges as one of the heroes of this epoch even though he led the unsuccessful Seventh Crusade and died during the eighth. His selflessness and purity of motive brought him abiding respect and eventual canonization.

For those who view history with a scorecard rather than a playbill, the final tally on the Crusades is harsh and inescapable. Seven of the nine were abject failures. The Children's Crusade is alleged to have caused the death or enslavement of thirty thousand youths. The Fourth Crusade saw the sacking of Constantinople by Western Christians, an act of perfidy that many blame for the continuing hostility of East toward West.

Only the First and Third Crusades provide Christian cheerleaders with much joy. And even those ventures were sometimes ignoble and the triumphs evanescent. By the dawn of the fourteenth century not an acre of territory recaptured in Palestine remained in Christian hands. True, the great shrines of the Holy Land stayed intact; but there is no persuasive evidence that the Turks or other Moslems would have desecrated or destroyed them.

There was silver periphery to the dark cloud of the Crusades. Words and concepts like "algebra" and "alchemy" entered the Western world, planting the seeds of science in a culture long controlled by a religious hierarchy. Architectural styles such as Romanesque and possibly Gothic are attributed to the influence from the Middle East. Special religious orders providing necessary services evolved, notably the Knights Templar (which instituted convoy security for unprotected travelers) and the Hospitallers of St. John (whose offering is implied in their title). The latter order survives today in several derivative forms whose anachronistic regalia and pomp are redeemed by their institutional succor to the infirm.

At their best, the Crusades were a courageous and selfless trek and mission toward a mystical goal that represented a place and a state of salvation. At their worst, they were the seven cardinal sins cloaked in Christendom's most cherished symbol.

Good or bad, the Crusades provide an extraordinary view of human nobility and human frailty and should be studied by every youth, especially those headed for the ministry or the military. Ignorance, arrogance, and power are a lethal mix, even in those with the best of intentions. And whether it is called "Jihad" or "Crusade," a holy war is almost always a contradiction in terms.

The Education Bay

The fourth bay on the left (north) side of the nave features education. The window, which depicts schools and colleges affiliated with the Episcopal Church, is the work of Willet Studios in Philadelphia. It was given by Mary Louise Moffatt in memory of her parents.

In **the rosette** 1, Christ as a youth is shown listening to the Temple doctors. The theme is completed in the rosette of the clerestory window far above where the youthful Christ is seen questioning and amazing those teachers.

The major diamonds in the left lancet read from bottom to top: 2 Trinity School, Manhattan; 3 King's College, Halifax, with Bishop Charles Inglis; 4 Hobart College, Geneva, N.Y., with Bishop John Henry Hobart; and 5 Trinity College, Hartford, Conn.

The small triangles on the sides contain seals of church-founded preparatory and parish schools in the Diocese of New York: 6 Trinity School in Pawling, N.Y.; 7 the Cathedral School, Manhattan (see the description under "The Cathedral Close," p. 149); 8 Greer School, Garrison, N.Y.; 9 St. Mary's School, Peekskill, N.Y.; 10 St. Thomas Choir School, Manhattan; and 11 the Malcolm Gordon School, Garrison, N.Y.

The major diamonds in the right lancet are: 12 Columbia University (originally King's College) with its founder, Samuel Johnson; 13 the doorway of General Theological Seminary, Manhattan; 14 Kenyon College with Bishop Philander Chase; and 15 the University of the South, with Bishop Leonidas Polk.

The small triangles on the sides of the right lancet complete the seals of preparatory and parish schools in the Diocese of New York: 16 Grace Church School, Manhattan; 17 St. Luke's School, Manhattan; 18 Church of the Heavenly Rest Day School, Manhattan; 19 St. Peter's School, Peekskill, N.Y.; 20 St. Hilda's and St. Hugh's School, Manhattan;

21 St. Luke's Hospital School of Nursing, Manhattan. (Note that the window of All Souls' Bay was the gift of the alumnae of this school, formerly located across 113th Street from the Cathedral.)

In **the triangles at the bottom corners of the lancets** are educational symbols (the first three dating back to Greek mythology): 22 a lyre, emblematic of fine arts; 23 an owl (symbol of wisdom) over a university door; 24 the caduceus, superimposed on the cross, representing medicine and nursing; 25 the spinning wheel, representing basic education imparted through homemaking.

 *Commentary*

Faith and Knowledge

The Education Bay is one of fourteen in the Cathedral's nave, putting education on a par with law, art, medicine, communications, religious life, etc. Meanwhile, a few hundred yards to the northwest is Columbia University with fifty-four departments. One of them, the Department of Religion, covers Christianity and all other major faiths.

At first blush, the priorities of these two institutions seem to be in sharp conflict. Is education one of many shared endeavors under the Christian canopy? Or is religion a subset of education, along with statistics, engineering, and South Asian studies?

The tension between religion (faith) and education (knowledge) is a longstanding tug-of-war. For centuries religion seemed to be winning. "Winning," of course, included suppression of Copernicus's heliocentric theory and the forced recantation of Galileo. It also meant consolidating the ranks by killing such independent thinkers as John Hus.

Finally the taut rope was yanked in the opposite direction. The Renaissance, as its name implies, was a rebirth of exploration with a new attitude toward learning. Freedom of inquiry and exploration spawned enlightenment and progress. The Reformation brought creativity to worship and a partial cleansing of the temple. Science blossomed and later brought forth the Industrial Revolution. It must have seemed to many like a story with a happy ending.

But the rope had been pulled too far in the new direction. The comfort and progress of some people entailed the subjugation of others. Slavery was rife in "enlightened" nations; and the Industrial Revolution came at the expense of "dark satanic mills," child labor, and the pollution of air, land, and water.

Knowledge had conferred genuine gifts on society — particularly in medicine, transportation, and communication. But in the euphoria of success, humankind declared itself the measure of all things and the controller of its own destiny. Two world wars have revealed the tragedy of this self-enthronement. And in their aftermath have come a welter of social and environmental problems. There is also a pervasive malaise of spirit, well-captured in the terse titles of modern writings: *The Wasteland, The Fall, No Exit, Lord of the Flies, The Age of Anxiety.*

Cathedral School scene

Ross Lewis

Is it time for the tug-of-war to lurch back toward religion? That prospect is unattractive in view of the past record. Furthermore, religion no longer speaks with a monolithic voice. Some leaders feel that prayer in the public schools is a high priority matter. Some believe that a wholesale redistribution of the world's wealth is essential to righteousness and survival. Birth control and abortion divide religious people and communions. And the proper response to perceived military threat is equally divisive among church folk.

The tension between religion and education may have served some purpose in the past as a corrective to presumption and excess on either side; but it is now an outmoded paradigm. Realizing this, a few leaders in religion and education have (a) acknowledged the limitations of their own spheres; (b) developed a respect for the contributions of each other; and (c) sought ways in which they can pull together on the same end of the rope against the seemingly intractable challenges of our time.

Science's province is the facts of life; religion's is the meaning of life. It is when one invades the territory of the other that the troubles begin. If religion has seemed to retreat in the last few centuries, it is only because it had pontificated on cosmology or evolution and claimed factual knowledge on the basis of divine revelation. Equally unfortunate has been the assumption on the part of some members of the scientific community that what cannot be seen, verified, or measured is nonexistent or unimportant.

A study of comparative religions can be worthwhile for a number of reasons, but it has no more relationship to the venture of faith than the study of recipes has to the eating of food. It is the *study*, not the *practice*, of religion that is properly slotted with other studies at the university.

When it comes to religious belief and practice, however, all other activities should be subordinate, since religion reflects our ultimate concern and represents the values by which all else is measured. Hence the rosettes atop each clerestory window of the Cathedral in which Christ reigns over the various professions and disciplines that constitute our common life. It was in this spirit that the medieval church developed the quadrivium in which the major liberal arts (arithmetic, geometry, astronomy, and music) came within the Summa of the Christian Faith. Chartres spawned its own university, while in Paris Notre Dame gave birth to the Sorbonne.

The basic priorities that took shape in medieval cathedrals still abide. Time and progress have not rendered them obsolete. The people of eight centuries ago knew nothing about galaxies, black holes, microbes, or DNA. But they knew that the earth was the Lord's and that their Redeemer lived. Their beliefs placed earthly life and death in a larger context, projected a vision of God against the great unknown, acknowledged alienation from that God and sought forgiveness and reconciliation.

Because our nation is pluralistic and has a constitutional separation of church and state, these matters are not part of the public school experience. Thus the emergence of private religious schools like those portrayed in the lancets of the Education window. Episcopal schools, among the earliest in the United States, have long since been outnumbered by Roman Catholic schools. Also part of the parochial school scene are Protestant, Evangelical, Jewish, and Muslim schools. Many religious schools are closing, and most of them are struggling as the twentieth century ends. Society as a whole will suffer if that trend continues. The comments of an inner-city parochial school principal, Sister June Favata, St. Vincent Academy, Newark, N.J., are cogent in this regard:

"When I first came here my goal was to provide as good an education as the children in suburbia receive and thereby propel my disadvantaged kids into the cultural mainstream. I soon realized that we lacked the funds for laboratories, field trips, sporting equipment, and those other extras that prosperous public school districts can afford. I was truly depressed to think that most of my kids were destined to remain in a subculture.

"But the more I looked at that mainstream, the more materialism, selfishness, and self-destruction I saw in it. Suddenly it occurred to me that our little school had resources that were unavailable to any public schools — beliefs, creeds and a value system. It was within our capacity to create a subculture superior to the mainstream. After all, that is what Christianity had been at the beginning. So now I have a new goal, and it is constantly energizing."

There is no hope of building and sustaining a better world without a fusion of faith and knowledge. Surely this is inherent in the two commandments proclaimed separately by the ancient Hebrews and combined by Jesus Christ, "Thou shalt love the Lord thy God with all thy heart, soul, mind, and strength — and thy neighbor as thyself."

The Law Bay

One of the six chapels of the nave is located in the Law Bay and is dedicated to St. Yves (sometimes spelled Ives), the patron of lawyers. The lower portion is dominated by a memorial to William Mercer Grosvenor, first dean of the Cathedral Church. The altar and the foot-pace on which it rests are of French Antique Rouge and Rose Numidian marble. In the center of the altar is a medallion carved with the symbol of the Revelation according to St. John the Divine: the lamb carrying the banner charged with the Cross and standing upon the Book of the Seven Seals.

The Reredos

The reredos (the screen behind and above the altar), carved in walnut by Pellegrini of Irving and Casson of Boston, is in the form of a triptych (see p. 54). It presents law-givers of the Old and New Testaments and many from subsequent generations who have lived under those laws. The pattern, although logical and symmetrical, does not lend itself to the customary left-to-right reading. And since the reredos was created by a different artist than the iconographer of the stained-glass window above it, there is a certain amount of repetition.

At the base of the reredos are 1 Adam and Eve receiving the Law in the Garden of Eden, and 2 Adam and Eve being expelled from the Garden for having transgressed the Law. Between those scenes is a panel 3 showing the youthful Jesus arguing the Law with the doctors of the Temple. At the extremes of the reredos base are 4 a kneeling Dean Grosvenor and 5 a representation of the Cathedral. On the four principal supports of the reredos are the symbols of the four Evangelists 6 Matthew, 7 Mark, 8 Luke, and 9 John.

In **the main section** of the reredos is 10 Jesus holding the Bible. It depicts the first part of his summary of the Law: "Thou shalt love the Lord thy God. . . ." Above 11 is the seated figure of the Judge of all people. To the left 12 is Moses, lawgiver of the Old Testament, above which is 13 the symbol of the burning bush through which God spoke to Moses (Exod. 3:2). To the right is 14 St. Paul, the great interpreter of the New Law; above 15 is a scene showing St. Paul and St. Timothy, his most frequent companion in spreading the Gospel.

The left door of the triptych represents three people who lived under the Law of Moses: 16 Samuel, above which is 17 the scene of Samuel judging Israel; 18 King David above which 19 he is shown composing Psalm 96; and 20 St. John the Baptist, with 21 his baptizing of Jesus portrayed above.

The rightmost portion of the triptych presents three who lived under the Law that emerged in the New Testament: 22 St. Ambrose, over which 23 he is shown rebuking the Emperor Theodosius for the massacre at Thessalonica; 24 St. Edward the Confessor, with a scene above 25 showing him canceling the Danegeld payments; and 26 St. Benedict beneath 27 the Abbey of Monte Casino.

In **the spired niches** over the central section are 28 the Virgin Mary and Child Jesus; 29 St. Anne, mother of the Virgin Mary, and 30 St. Elizabeth, the Virgin's cousin. In the niche to the left at the top is 31 St. Joachim, husband of St. Anne; and matching it on the right is 32 St. Zacharias, husband of St. Elizabeth and father of John the Baptist. Beneath Joachim are 33 St. Yves, patron of lawyers, flanked by 34 Sibyl Agrippa and 35 Sibyl Erythraea. Correspondingly, on the right is 36 St. Philogonius, who defended the faith against the Arian heresy. Flanking this figure are 37 Sibyl Perseca and 38 Sibyl Phrygia.*

Finally, **the carved statues** on the four principal supports of the central section are 39 Aristotle (384–322 B.C.E.) with 40 Alexander Hamilton (1755–1804) above; 41 Plato (428–348 B.C.E.) with 42 Hugo Grotius (1583–1645) above; 43 Abu Hanifa (died 767 C.E.) with 44 Immanuel Kant (1724–1804) above; and 45 Mencius (371–289 B.C.E.) with 46 John Marshall (1755–1835) above.

There were twelve Sibyls, priestesses of Apollo in the polytheistic Greek religion. They were thought by many to have prophesied the events in the life of Jesus from his birth to his Resurrection.

The hand-carved Law reredos

Joe Trimble

The Law Window

The window that rises behind the Grosvenor Memorial in the Law Bay was made by Wilbur Herbert Burnham.

[1] **The rosette** features two angels with St. Ambrose (339–97), scholar, lawyer, preacher, bishop of Milan, and one of the four Latin doctors of the church. He was a major opponent of Arianism which had challenged the triune nature of God. In the spandrels are figures representing [2] Law and [3] Justice.

The major medallions of the left lancet: [4] the Handwriting on the Wall (Dan. 5:25); [5] the Judgment of Solomon — in which the wise king restored an infant to its mother (1 Kings 3:16–28); [6] Moses and the Tablets of the Law (Exod. 20:1–17); [7] Adam and Eve receiving the Law from God (Gen. 3:1–19).

The border medallions are: [8] Hammurabi receiving his code from the sun god (eighteenth century B.C.E.); [9] Edward I of England (1239–1307) dismissing corrupt judges; [10] Solon, Greek lawmaker (sixth century B.C.E.) interpreting the oracle of Delphi; [11] Henry II of England arguing with Archbishop Thomas Becket over the question of the king's court versus the ecclesiastical court; [12] Ulpianus Domitius, Roman jurist (born circa 170 C.E.); [13] Godfrey de Bouillon, Crusader and founder of the code of Jerusalem.

The major medallions of the right lancet: [14] The Justinian Code, named for the Roman emperor and lawmaker (483–565); [15] King John of England signing the Magna Carta in 1215 (see the Magna Carta pedestal in the sanctuary, p. 130). [16] the Mayflower Covenant, a compact drawn by those disembarking from the *Mayflower* at Cape Cod in 1620; [17] the Constitution of the United States, the basis of U.S. law as approved in Philadelphia in 1787.

The border medallions: [18] Henry de Bracton, chancellor of Exeter Cathedral, writing his treatise, *Laws and Customs of England;* [19] Napoleon, in 1804, dictating the code that would secure the gains of the French Revolution; [20] Hugo Grotius (1583–1645), Dutch artist and statesman, stressing freedom of the seas (*mare liberum*); [21] Joseph Story (1779–1845), professor of law at Harvard University; [22] George Zabriskie, first chancellor of the Episcopal Diocese of New York; [23] John Marshall (1755–1835), fourth chief justice of the United States and a founder of American common law.

At the bases of the two lancets are the following symbols: [24] the Law of Nature, suggested by the sun; [25] the Wheel of Justice, representing mystic power; [26] Civil Law, symbolized by the fasces (a bundle of rods tied around an axe); and [27] Justice, marked by a set of scales.

The rosette in this window was given in memory of John Paul Herren by his wife, Emma Banks Herren. The lancets are in memory of Ephraim Squire Force and Sara Jane Force, given by their daughter, Caroline.

The Anglican History Bay

The dominant theme of the sixth bay on the north aisle is English Christianity, though there are some Irish, Welsh, Scottish, and American figures as well. For a summary of Christianity throughout the British Isles, please see "Anglican/Episcopal Tradition: A Brief History," pp. 155–159.

1 St. Columba (521–97) is shown in **the rosette** along with St. Gregory the Great who as pope (590–604) dispatched Augustine to Canterbury. The third figure is St. Theodore of Tarsus who became the seventh archbishop of Canterbury (668–92). The tracery pieces feature 2 Noah and 3 the Virgin Mary.

Strangely, all four of **the major medallions of the left lancet** present saints who are pictured elsewhere in the same window: 4 St. Theodore of Tarsus; 5 St. Augustine, first archbishop of Canterbury;

6 St. Columba; and 7 St. Joseph of Arimathea.

The minor medallions of the left lancet are: 8 St. Cuthbert of Durham, with the head of King Oswald; 9 St. Swithin, bishop of Winchester; 10 St. David, bishop of Menevia and patron of Wales; 11 St. Patrick, patron of Ireland, shown with a shamrock and a snake at his feet; 12 St. Andrew the Apostle, patron of Scotland; 13 St. George, patron of England, shown slaying the dragon.

The major medallions of the right lancet are: 14 the founding of Westminster Abbey by St. Edward the Confessor; 15 Drake's Bay, where the Prayer Book was first used for worship in the Western Hemisphere; 16 Jamestown, Virginia, where the Prayer Book was first used regularly in the Western Hemisphere; 17 St. Joseph of Arimathea, the New Testament personage who is alleged to have brought the Holy Grail (the chalice used at the Last Supper) to Glastonbury, England. This became the basis of the noble quest attributed to King Arthur and his knights several centuries later.

The minor medallions of the right lancet read: 18 Bishop Thomas Ken (1637–1711), who wrote the Doxology; 19 Bishop Daniel Sylvester Tuttle, pioneer to the American West; 20 Lanfranc, who served as thirty-fifth archbishop of Canterbury (1070–93) and started rebuilding the cathedral into its present form; 21 John Cosin (1594–1672), bishop of Durham, builder of many churches, hospices, and libraries; 22 St. Friedewide (680–735), princess and abbess, patron of Christ Church Cathedral, Oxford; 23 St. Ethelreda (630?–679), a Northumbrian queen who gave up her crown to become an abbess.

At the bases of the two lancets are four quarter circles in which are shown the four Latin doctors of the church: 24 St. Jerome, 25 St. Ambrose, 26 St. Augustine of Hippo, and 27 St. Gregory.

The entire bay, including the clerestory window above, was given by Edgar Palmer in memory of David Palmer, Mary Katharine Squires Palmer, and Susan Flanders Palmer. The windows were made by Wilbur Herbert Burnham.

The American History Bay

The easternmost bay of the north aisle celebrates events and personages in American history. At floor level are the effigy, tomb, and chantry of William Thomas Manning, tenth bishop of New York. It is an appropriate place for that eminent prelate, since it epitomizes his tireless and imaginative fundraising efforts to complete the Cathedral's nave. The tomb was carved from Carrara marble by Constantin Antonovici.

Originally Bishop Manning designated this alcove as "The Historical and Patriotic Societies' Bay" and sought support from organizations ranging from the Daughters of the American Revolution to small groups of ethnic immigrants from eastern Europe. Had this campaign succeeded, the window would probably have placed greater emphasis on the melting-pot, polyglot character of our nation. The window, made by Ernest W. Lakeman, was actually given by the family of John Jacob Astor, whose death on the *Titanic* is depicted in the lower right corner of the right lancet.

As a link with our Anglican origins and ties, **the rosette** 1 shows St. Alban, England's protomartyr, and the tracery pieces present 2 the Magna Carta (1215) and 3 the Liberty Bell (1776).

The major medallions of the left lancet: 4 the capture of Quebec by British commander James Wolfe (1759), 5 the Declaration of Independence (1776), 6 the inauguration of George Washington (1789), 7 Thomas Jefferson and the Louisiana Purchase (1803).

The minor medallions: 8 Stephen Langton, forty-fourth archbishop of Canterbury, whose influence helped bring the Magna Carta into being and who is also credited with dividing the books of the Bible into chapters; 9 Christopher Columbus, Italian explorer who sailed under the Spanish flag (1492); 10 John Cabot, Italian explorer who sailed under the English flag (1497); 11 Captain John Smith, English soldier who founded the Colony of Virginia; 12 Benjamin Franklin, publisher, inventor, statesman, and founding father of the nation; 13 Alexander Hamilton, statesman, first Secretary of the Treasury, and founding father.

The major medallions of the right lancet: 14 the Battle of Lake Erie (War of 1812); 15 Lincoln's Gettysburg Address (1863); 16 the return of soldiers from the Spanish American War (1898); 17 the signing of the armistice after World War I (1918).

The minor medallions: 18 Daniel Webster, Northern nineteenth-century statesman; 19 John Calhoun, Southern nineteenth-century statesman; 20 Oliver Wendell Holmes, outstanding American jurist; 21 Henry Clay, political leader who sought compromise between the North and the South prior to the Civil War; 22 Henry Adams, nineteenth-century historian; 23 Elihu Root, senator, diplomat, cabinet member, and an active supporter of this Cathedral.

The four corners at **the base** of the two lancets offer 24 Henry Hudson, explorer; 25 Betsy Ross, who is credited with sewing the first American flag; 26 Francis Scott Key, who wrote the "Star Spangled Banner" during the War of 1812; and 27 the sinking of the *Titanic* (1912).

Bishop Manning's effigy

G. Lynas

All Souls' Bay

The first bay on the right (south) side of the nave honors the service and the souls of the departed. Two themes are interwoven in the window and altar of All Souls' Bay: the Corporal Works of Mercy (service to our needy fellow human beings) and Paradise (the ultimate triumph of Christ and the faithful). The polychrome reredos pictured on page 61, focuses only on Christ and the saints. But above is a stained-glass window in which biblical heroes are flanked by references to contemporary humanitarian agencies, especially those supported by the Diocese of New York. Not all are still functioning and some have changed their name or thrust. But that is the inevitable consequence when current entities are permanently enshrined.

The window was given by the alumnae of the School of Nursing of St. Luke's Hospital. It was designed and made by Otto Heinigke and Loris Withers. The chart identifying the window panels has been numbered in accordance with the wishes of the iconographers.

1 **The rosette** presents the seal of St. Luke's Hospital. The curved triangles or tracery on the sides show 2 the ship symbol of St. Nicholas, with the caduceus below, and 3 the "George" from the badge of the Order of the Garter, with a brazen serpent below. Thus is the overall theme of healing established.

The left lancet starts at the apex 4 with the healing of Peter's wife's mother, flanked by 4A Florence Nightingale nursing a wounded soldier in the Crimean War and 4B the Elko Lake Camp of the Diocese of New York's Episcopal Mission Society. 5 Elijah meeting the widow of Zarapath is flanked by 5A services to the aged and 5B St. Barnabas House. 6 The feeding of the five thousand is flanked by 6A the Department of Christian Social Relations and 6B Clara Barton founding the American Red Cross. 7 The Parable of the Good Samaritan has at its sides 7A the House of the Holy Comforter and 7B the Episcopal Churchwomen. 8 Jesus and the Samaritan woman at the well are between 8A a Market Cross and 8B the celebration of the Holy Eucharist.

The right lancet commences at the apex with 9 the Sermon on the Mount flanked by 9A the work of the Youth Consultation Service and 9B St. Mary's-in-the-Field in Valhalla, N.Y. 10 The healing of the centurion's servant is shown between 10A St. Ann's School for the Deaf and 10B a patient at St. Luke's Hospital. 11 St. Paul, St. Silas, and St. Luke are welcomed by St. Lydia. On either side are 11A the Seaman's Church Institute and 11B other services for immigrants and visitors. 12 St. Peter, being delivered from prison by an angel, is flanked by 12A Westfield State Farm and 12B a prison chaplain from the Episcopal Mission Society. 13 The entombment of Christ has at its sides 13A the burying ground of St. George's Society and 13B the performance of the Burial Office.

Young choristers in front of polychromed reredos in All Souls' Bay

The All Souls' Altar and Reredos

The altar is made of yellow Lamartene marble. Behind and above the altar is a screen (called "reredos") divided into three sections. Carvings at the top of the center section show Christ crucified, with the Virgin Mary and St. John on either side forming what is called the "Holy Rood." The niches on the left have St. Luke and St. Peter; to the right are St. Paul and John the Baptist.

Beneath the carvings, the theme of Paradise has been portrayed by Leo Cartwright in a polychromed painting. In the center panel, Christ the King is surrounded by angels and archangels. The lilies at his feet represent divine purity and the vine and branches represent his relationship to his followers. The figures in the two side panels are identified below.

The central figure in **the left panel** is [1] the Virgin Mary with stars in her nimbus (halo) as described in Revelation. Also shown are [2] St. John the Evangelist with the book of his Gospel; [3] St. Joseph with the flowering staff; [4] St. Edward the Confessor with scepter and ring; [5] St. Mary Magdalene with the jar of ointment; [6] St. Veronica with the veil; [7] St. Elizabeth of Hungary with two children and the bread that symbolizes her charity; [8] St. Anthony with a Tau cross on his shoulders; [9] St. Stephen holding the stones of his martyrdom; [10] St. Bernardino in Franciscan habit; [11] St. Joan of Arc with the fleur-de-lis; [12] St. Thomas Becket with his pastoral staff and a wound in his head; [13] St. Gregory the Great with papal tiara and dove; [14] and St. Cecilia with a crown of red and white roses.

On **the right panel** we see [15] St. Margaret of Scotland with a black cross; [16] St. David of Wales with a model of the Cathedral of Menevia; [17] St. Martin with sword and cloak; [18] St. Ursula with three young virgins, one of whom holds an arrow, symbol of their martyrdom; [19] St. Francis of Assisi, the central figure in this panel, with a bird in one hand and stigmata in

the other; [20] St. Gery of Cambrai in episcopal vestments holding a broken manacle; [21] St. Clare with a cross of palm leaves; [22] St. Jerome as a cardinal; [23] St. Thomas Aquinas with a symbol of the sun with an eye in the center; [24] St. Catherine with a broken wheel; [25] St. George with a red cross; [26] St. Paul holding a sword; [27] St. Giles in Benedictine habit; [28] St. Luke with pen and Gospel; [29] and St. Peter of Alcantara with a star above his head.

 *Commentary*

Saints: Heroes of the Faith

To those of us who did not grow up in a milieu of churchly saints, the figures in stone and stained-glass seem remote, alien, or unreal. Our first introduction to many of their names may be through sports headlines. Thus we come to realize that "Bonnies Trounce Macs" indicates that the school team from St. Bonaventure has soundly defeated its rival at Immaculate Conception. But Bonaventure himself is part of the misty past. We know nothing about the person or most of the other nineteen hundred names on the calendar of saints.

Or we may know just enough to question the whole practice of designating saints. There are some valid criticisms of this longtime tradition. Many saints were born to privilege, material, educational, or both. Does canonization, therefore, honor those who were already lucky by birth? A vast majority of saints were priests, monks, or nuns, and even those from the laity were usually unmarried. Is this a club in which single people keep honoring singleness? Then there is the need to prove that a candidate accomplished observable, verifiable miracles — another stumbling block for those who believe that the great miracles are those transformations within the human heart.

The process may be flawed or moot, and it may overlook some of God's most faithful servants. Still, it has yielded an outstanding collection of human beings, heroes of the faith, heroes vastly superior in character to those usually chosen by secular society.

Secular society canonizes in haste and repents at leisure. Achievers in entertainment, sports, and business are quickly elevated to the rank of heroes and become role models before their clay feet have been revealed. In New York, a young man used a gun to shoot at subway hoodlums; he became the toast of the town until we took a second look. Nationally, a

handsome lad made a solo flight across the Atlantic and became enshrined in our collective heart until he later showed Nazi sympathies.

The populace, young and old, would do well to reconsider its priorities and look for inspiration to those whose achievements and values have withstood the test of time. It need not be a dreary quest, especially for those who start with Phyllis McGinley's charming, thoughtful book, *Saint Watching* (New York: Crossroad, 1982).

Meanwhile, the following chart may be helpful in providing basic information on a few of the most celebrated saints since the New Testament era. The designation of "Doctor" has been awarded to only thirty-one saints in all of history. It honors those who have contributed to Christian doctrine and thought.

	Feast Day	Symbol	Role
Thomas Aquinas 1225–1274	Jan 28	A book radiating light	Doctor; wrote "Summa Theologica"
Catherine of Siena 1347–1380	Apr 29	Heart with Cross	Doctor; helped return papacy to Rome
Augustine of Canterbury ?–604	May 27	Bishop's miter	First Archbishop of Canterbury
Joan of Arc 1412–1431	May 30	Coat of armor	Martyr; rallied French forces
Boniface 675–754	Jun 6	A felled tree	Martyr (see chapel)
Columba 521–597	Jun 9	Abbot's habit	Founded Iona Abbey (see chapel)
Anthony of Padua 1195–1231	Jun 13	Lily (purity)	Doctor; servant of the poor and sick
Benedict 480–550	Jul 11	"Ausculta fili"	Founder and framer of western monasticism
Bonaventure 1221–1274	Jul 15	"O buona ventura"	Doctor; reconciled Christian factions
Ignatius Loyola 1491–1556	Jul 31	"Ad Majorem Dei Gloriam"	Founded Society of Jesus (Jesuits)
Dominic 1170–1221	Aug 8	Black cloak; white robe	Founded Dominicans; developed the Rosary
Bernard of Clairvaux 1091–1153	Aug 20	Chained Devil	Doctor; strengthened Cistercian order
Augustine of Hippo 354–430	Aug 28	Broken heart (penitence)	Doctor; bishop; wrote "Confessions"
Gregory the Great 540–604	Sep 3	Papal tiara	Doctor; reformed calendar and liturgy
Jerome 341–420	Sep 30	Lion	Doctor; translated Bible into Latin
Francis of Assisi 1181–1226	Oct 4	Wolf; birds; stigmata	Patron of nature; foremost friar
Teresa of Avila 1515–1582	Oct 15	Flaming dart	Doctor; reformed Carmelite Order
Ambrose 339–397	Dec 7	Swarm of bees	Doctor (see chapel)

The Missionary Bay

The iconographers of the arcade window stated that they had taken decorative inspiration from windows in Chartres and Canterbury. Blue predominates in the major and minor medallions, which are, in turn, set in Gothic leaf motifs in which rich rubies prevail.

[1] **The rosette** presents the Great Commission: Christ sends his Apostles into the world.

The major medallions of the left lancet are as follows: [2] St. Barnabas is shown holding the Gospel of Mark and preaching; [3] St. Cyril and St. Methodius, Greek monks and missionaries to the Slavic nations along the banks of the Danube, are shown preaching to the king of Bulgaria; [4] St. Patrick, patron saint of Ireland, is shown preaching; [5] St. Columba preaches to the Picts on the island of Iona, where he established a monastery in 563 C.E.

The minor medallions of the left lancet are: [6] St. Vladimir, grand duke of Kiev, who introduced Christianity to Russia; [7] St. Sergius, patriarch of Constantinople; [8] St. Isaac Jogues, Jesuit priest to Native Americans in the Huron Mission, martyred during this ministry; [9] William Carey, scholar and pioneer of modern missionary endeavor, preaching to Hindus in India; [10] Jackson Kemper, bishop of Missouri and Indiana, administering the Holy Communion; [11] David Livingstone, famed explorer and missionary, holding the Bible and preaching to Africans.

The major medallions of the right lancet are: [12] St. Willibrord, Apostle to the Frisians and bishop of Utrecht, converting tribes of northern Europe; [13] St. Boniface, Benedictine monk and patron saint of Germany, preaching to the German tribes; [14] St. Ulfilas, Apostle of the Goths, for whom he translated the Bible; [15] St. Paul with the magicians of Ephesus, who converted and burned their books of sorcery before him.

The minor medallions of the right lancet: [16] James Hannington, heroic missionary, martyr, and first bishop of Eastern Equatorial Africa; [17] Henry Martyn, who translated the New Testament into Hindustani, Arabic, and Persian; [18] St. Francis Xavier, in his Jesuit robe, portrayed converting two Chinese; [19] Bartolomé de Las Casas, missionary, Dominican friar, and bishop of Chiapas, Mexico; [20] Philander Chase, bishop of Ohio (where he is shown laying the cornerstone of Kenyon College) and later of Illinois; [21] St. Nicholai, Eastern Orthodox archbishop and missionary to the Japanese.

Across **the base** of the two lancets are four Episcopal missionaries in the western United States, each kneeling in prayer: [22] Henry Benjamin Whipple, bishop of Minnesota; [23] William Hobart Hare, bishop of South Dakota; [24] Hudson Stuck, missionary to Alaska; [25] Daniel Sylvester Tuttle, bishop of Montana and sometime presiding bishop of the Church in North America.

Designed and made by Wilbur Herbert Burnham, this window was given by Francis M. Whitehouse as a memorial to Henry John Whitehouse (1803–74), bishop of Illinois.

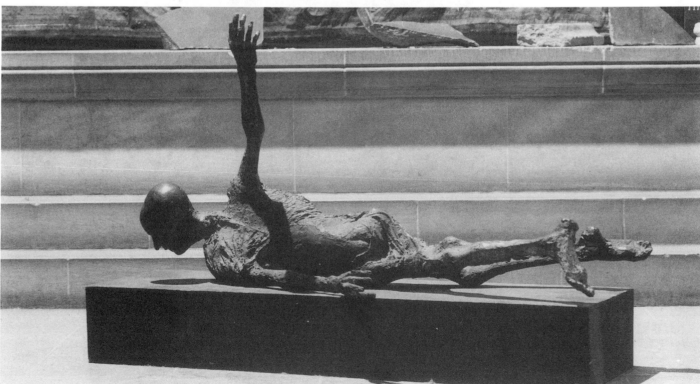

Armenian Memorial and Holocaust Memorial in Missionary Bay

G. Lynas

[64]

Westward view during the winter solstice observance.

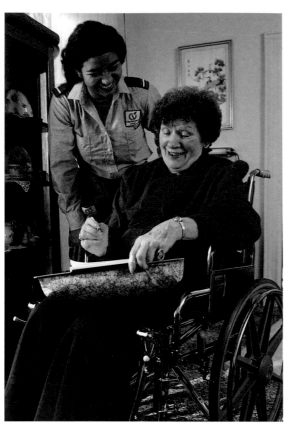

Lead stone cutter Angel Escobar and apprentice Lisa Young in the Cathedral Stoneyard.

The Cathedral's outreach programs attend those who cannot attend church.

James Parks Morton, the seventh and longest-serving of the Cathedral's deans.

Traditional gargoyle (left) and corbel honoring Nelson Mandela (right) by carver Emmanuel Fourchet.

The American History window, given in memory of John Jacob Astor, records the event of his death.

Environmentalist Al Gore joins clergy, animal lovers, and fellow fauna at the Feast of St. Francis.

Bishop Richard Grein and Cathedral musicians amid thousands of worshipers at the Feast of St. Francis.

Autumn view of the Cathedral Close with the south tower at two-thirds of its ultimate height.

The Labor Bay

The arcade window of the Labor Bay is one of the most varied and instructive in the entire church. Two themes are interwoven with symmetrical use of brilliant colors. The main medallions of blue present the two biblical Josephs (the patriarchal dreamer in the left lancet, the guardian of the Holy Family in the right). Surrounding them in red are examples of vocations that enable and enrich our shared lives as a society. Hidden by the top of the arcade's tapestry is a medieval watchword, *Laborare est orare* (to work is to pray). In the left lancet is an instance of prefiguration (see commentary on p. 66). All in all, it is a space that speaks to everyone from biblical student to trade unionist.

1 In **the rosette,** St. Joseph is represented working at his carpenter's bench. Beside him is the youthful Jesus, symbolically bearing a yoke.

The principal medallions of the left lancet show the Joseph of the Old Testament: 2 relating his dream to his brothers; 3 being sold into slavery; 4 rising to become a ruler in Egypt; and 5 revealing himself to his brothers.

The irregular-shaped medallions on the side show ancient vocations: 6 the making of arrow heads; 7 Native Americans cultivating corn; 8 an Apostle mending nets; 9 medieval sawyers with a pit saw; 10 Romans making brick; and 11 a Phoenician cloth-dyer.

In **the right lancet,** dedicated to St. Joseph the Carpenter, we see those events in which he figured prominently. Like the left lancet, this is intended to read sequentially from top to bottom: 12 the espousal of Joseph and Mary; 13 the manger scene of the Nativity; 14 Joseph warned by an angel of Herod's intent and told to go to Egypt; and 15 the flight into Egypt.

On the side, **the irregular-shaped medallions** bring vocations up to the twentieth century: 16 the blacksmith, 17 the potter, 18 the printer, 19 the construction engineer, 20 the tapestry weaver, and 21 the cowboy herding cattle.

Across **the base** of the two lancets are 22 the cotton gin, 23 the glass blower, 24 the water wheel, 25 a clipper ship, 26 a farmer at mid-day rest, and 27 the first locomotive.

The Labor Bay is a memorial to Andrew Zabriskie given by his wife. The window is the work of Nicola D'Ascenzo.

 *Commentary*

Prototypes and Prefiguration

There was a popular medieval belief that the Old Testament was the New Testament concealed, and the New Testament was therefore the Old Testament revealed. Thus Jesus and Mary were prefigured by prototypes in the Law and the Prophets, and crucial events in the Gospels were foretold in the Torah.

From such a perspective, the brazen serpent of Moses foreshadows the Cross, and the three days spent by Jonah in the whale's belly anticipates the three days spent by Jesus in the tomb.

The citations are myriad. Some evoke admiration for the ingenuity of medieval exegetes. Others are compelling. If they do not persuade the modern mind, they at least suggest the possibility that portions of the New Testament (most notably Matthew's Gospel) were written to prove that Jesus was indeed the fulfillment of many scriptural prototypes.

With prefiguration in mind, re-examine the major medallions of the left lancet of the Labor Bay: [2] Joseph telling his brothers of his dream becomes the youthful Jesus astonishing the priests of the Temple; [3] Joseph being sold to the Ishmaelites for pieces of silver foretells Jesus being "sold out" by Judas for silver pieces; [4] Joseph's triumph over adversity and his rise to power prefigure the Resurrection; and [5] Joseph identifying himself to his nonrecognizing brothers is the typology for the risen Christ identifying himself to his distraught disciples near the road to Emmaus.

Firemen's Memorial in the Labor Bay

Cathedral Archives

Tapestry weaver and cowboy
from Labor Bay Window

The Communications Bay

The seated figure of St. John Chrysostom 1 occupies **the rosette.** The beehive symbolizes his eloquence as a preacher (honeyed words). Other symbols include chalice and cross (worship and faith), book (his homilies), and descending dove (the presence of the Holy Spirit). The tracery triangles show 2 St. George, legendary martyr of the early church, and 3 the dragon, which he is said to have slain.

The lancets are broadly chronological and should be read top to bottom, **left lancet** first: 4 Homer (twelfth century B.C.E.), teller of Greek legends such as *The Iliad* and *The Odyssey*, with a lyre at his feet, suggesting musical accompaniment; 5 a Stone Age man cutting a pictograph on the walls of his cave; 6 two tablets of the Ten Commandments; 7 a Babylonian making cuneiform tablets; 8 Manetho (third century B.C.E.) writing Egyptian chronicles; 9 an Egyptian carver; 10 a Mayan scribe; 11 Cadmus of Miletus, who created several of the letters in the Greek alphabet, some of which are shown beside his shoulders and waist; 12 a Chinese block printer; 13 a Roman workman cutting the letters S.P.Q.R. (Senate and People of Rome); 14 Charlemagne (742–814), discussing the revision of the Vulgate with the British scholar and theologian Alcuin; 15 an African tapping out a message on his war drum; 16 a Native American sending a smoke signal.

The right lancet celebrates communications of the last thousand years in which mechanical devices have made mass production possible: 17 Gutenberg (1398–1468), the father of printing in the Western world, inspecting a proof sheet for the first printing of the Bible; 18 a medieval monk illuminating a manuscript; 19 Aldus Manutius printing the first edition of *Virgil*; 20 Samuel F. B. Morse sending his first telegraphic message. (The young woman beside him is the daughter of Commissioner Ellsworth, who had chosen a biblical text as the first message: "What

hath God wrought," Num. 23:25.); 21 the printing of the Bay Psalm Book; 22 a wood engraver; 23 a linotype operator at work; 24 a telephone lineman keeping communications open; 25 a primitive television set presaging a new era in message-sending; 26 radio broadcasting depicted by a male violinist and a female holding a script (It is believed that Jack Benny and Mary Livingston were the prototypes; the presence of the two hemispheres symbolizes the worldwide scope of radio waves.); 27 a reporter typing his story, and within hours 28 a newsboy delivering it to the public. Three printers' marks are shown in the right lancet. The Kelmscott mark is in the left border, the St. Alban's mark is just below the wood engraver, 22 and the Aldus mark is included in niche 19 .

Commentary

Humankind, God, and Messages

If human beings could not communicate and interact with each other, they would scarcely qualify as fauna, much less as the most advanced of earth's species. Communication is the first rudiment of society.

Apart from vocal sounds, the drumbeats of Africa may have been the first community medium. Also dating back several millennia are the smoke signals of the Chinese, Assyrians, and Native Americans.

Since communication removes isolation and paves the way for creative interdependence, it is appropriate to note that most of its inventors were dependent on the work of others. Gutenberg's printing press was the product of a small team whose other members later sued for possession of the patent. Perhaps the Chinese should have sued the entire team, since they had already been printing books for centuries.

Samuel F. B. Morse, a painter-turned-inventor, drew heavily on the earlier works of fellow American Joseph Henry. Alexander Graham Bell built on the experiments of physicist Michael Faraday. Guglielmo Marconi expanded the experiments of his predecessors to produce wireless messages and then lived to see his efforts further expanded by others into radio.

Television had nineteenth-century progenitors in France, the United States, Germany, and Scotland. But it was Englishman John Baird who, in the 1920s, achieved kinetic results from the theories and groundwork of others. The plans for our Communications window were formulated at this time; and a foresighted iconographer designated a niche to celebrate this advance, which would not enter the public domain for another fifteen years.

The Judaeo-Christian tradition is rife with communications. God addressed a formless universe and called forth life, then thought briefly ("Let us make man in our own image"), and later warned Adam and Eve about forbidden fruit. Still later, God sent a technicolor peace sign to Noah, using the sky as a screen. God dictated Ten Commandments to Moses and climactically delivered the New Commandment through the Son, Jesus Christ.

The story of the life, death, and Resurrection of Jesus is called the Gospel (Godspell), or Good News. Hence in our Communication clerestory there are huge representations of two of the reporters of that news: St. Matthew and St. Mark. St. John proclaims the divinity of communication. "In the beginning was the Word...and the Word became flesh and dwelt among us." It is this Good News that has informed every worthy Christian sermon — from St. Peter to Phillips Brooks; from St. Paul to Dwight L. Moody; from St. John Chrysostom to Archbishop Tutu; from St. Francis to Cardinal Hume.

Preaching is often derogated, sometimes unfairly. "Deeds not words" is a frequent jibe of those who forget that words *are* deeds ("By thy words shalt thou be justified and by thy words condemned"). Others decry the impotence of words, oblivious to their own words (sometimes quite eloquent), which are undercutting the whole thesis.

It is sadly true that some messages of hate and divisiveness have often been cloaked in Christian symbols. The fact that the Good News has survived the ignorance and manipulation of fallible representatives through the centuries is one of its greatest validations. It is the light that no amount of darkness can extinguish.

Telephone line worker, Native American sending smoke signals and early television, from the Communications Bay window

The Medicine Bay

he fifth bay on the right (south) side of the nave honors the role of medicine in society. It is dedicated to St. Luke, the Beloved Physician.

The altar and the reredos by Irving and Casson of Boston are a memorial to the Reverend Dr. Reginald Heber Starr. The altar is of Hauteville marble; the reredos is hand-carved English oak. Beneath the statue of St. Luke are three panels depicting the raising of the son of the widow of Nain, the Gospels of the four Evangelists, and the Parable of the Good Samaritan (which appears only in St. Luke's Gospel).

Since November 9, 1985, there has been a memorial in this bay to those whose deaths came from Acquired Immune Deficiency Syndrome. A memorial book, listing the names of thousands who have died of AIDS, is invariably surrounded by votive candles placed by survivors in memory of loved ones. The Cathedral seeks to reach out to AIDS sufferers in the manner that Christ reached out to lepers.

The stained-glass window, made by Reynolds, Francis, and Rohnstock, is in the style of one of the earliest medieval windows with circular and semicircular medallions. **The rosette** shows ① the triumphant Christ on a foliated Cross, suggested by the text, "the leaves of the tree were for the healing of the nations." On each side are kneeling angels, one holding a chalice (cup), the other a sudarium (napkin).

The major medallions of the two lancets show the healing miracles of Christ. On **the left:** ② healing the deaf and dumb; ③ healing the lame man; ④ healing the infirm woman; and ⑤ healing the lepers.

On **the right:** ⑥ the raising of Lazarus; ⑦ casting out the devils; ⑧ healing the palsied man; and ⑨ raising the daughter of Jairus.

In **the semicircular medallions** are shown some of the leading figures in medical history. Starting at the bottom of **the left lancet:** ⑩ Imhotep, the Egyptian priest (twenty-sixth century B.C.E.) and first person identified with curative processes, whose name has become a greeting of well-wishing, particularly among people of color; ⑪ Hippocrates, Greek physician (fifth century B.C.E.), often called the Father of Modern Medicine (a huge representation of him also appears in the clerestory window far above); 12 Galen, who conducted anatomical studies in Rome, shown dissecting a Barbary ape; just to the left, in the lancet border, is a human skeleton, a tribute to the value of the X-ray in the diagnostic process; 13 Paul of Aegina, the Byzantine, shown working on his encyclopedia of medical knowledge; 14 Avicenna, the Arab, who introduced herbs and drugs to the curing and healing process; and finally, 15 one of the Knights Hospitaller of St. John of Jerusalem, an order that emerged during the Crusades.

In **the right lancet** we have, 16 Louis Pasteur drawing the first picture of a microbe; 17 Joseph Lister using antiseptic on a wound; 18 Father Damien, missionary to the lepers of Molokai; 19 Dr. William T. G. Norton, the Boston dentist who first performed a painless surgical operation using ether, the only American shown in this window. Finally, two celebrated nurses: 20 Florence Nightingale, who served in the Crimean War (Her memorial service in 1925 brought a procession of 2400 nurses down the center aisle of this half-completed cathedral): and 21 Edith Cavell, the martyred English nurse. Those who miss Clara Barton will find her portrayed in the window of All Souls' Bay.

In **the quarter circles** in the bottom corners of the lancets are 22 a chemist at work, 23 a nurse with a patient, 24 a country doctor in his gig, and 25 Pasteur inoculating a sheep. In the lower left corner of the left lancet a person seeks the "healing jewel," once believed to be in the head of a toad.

 *Commentary*

Curing and Healing

"To your health, wealth, and happiness," goes the time-honored toast. Is that the best we can wish for a friend or loved one? Hard to say without a definition of terms. Happiness could mean vapid hedonism; wealth could mean the ultimate in gluttony; and health could mean nothing more than the absence of annoying symptoms.

Health is the focus of these paragraphs as we consider curing and healing. We will arbitrarily define "curing" as the removing of symptoms and "healing" as the achievement of wholeness, a psychosomatic harmony, an inner peace. The two are

quite different but not mutually exclusive. Both elements seem to have been present in the miracles of Christ.

Curing without healing can be seen in caricature in advertisements for aspirin and antacids as the antidote for headaches and upset stomachs. The mind and body are sending out systemic signals and the cure merely erases them temporarily.

However, a preponderance of the advances in medical science are seen by a vast majority of the populace as a boon to humankind. Within the lifetime of all senior citizens, poliomyelitis was a major scourge in society. This as well as scarlet fever and small pox have been conquered in the twentieth century. Diagnostic techniques and equipment have prolonged countless lives. Pharmaceutical progress has put such maladies as epilepsy under control.

The church in its finite wisdom has sometimes resisted the contributions of medical science. More often, it has welcomed the medical world as a partner in the restoration of health. Some of New York's foremost hospitals — St. Luke's, Mt. Sinai, St. Vincent's, and Presbyterian Medical Centers — are the creations and continuing concerns of major religious groups. It is also worth noting that some of the most celebrated physicians in history were devoutly religious: Dr. Albert Schweitzer, Dr. David Livingstone, St. Luke, Dr. Wilfred Grenfell, and Dr. Tom Dooley.

There is probably no other church that honors as many men and women of medicine as those portrayed in the window of our Medicine Bay. However, there is a statue of Edward Jenner (developer of vaccines) in Gloucester Cathedral; Sir Arthur Flemming (discoverer of penicillin) is entombed at St. Paul's Cathedral; and even Sigmund Freud has won latter-day homage in the stained glass of Grace Cathedral in San Francisco.

Any discussion of religion and healing must take respectful note of a powerful nineteenth-century leader, Mary Baker Eddy. The Christian Science fellowship, which she established, puts total emphasis on faith and prayer and the attainment of inner health.

In an era when physical sciences were beginning to seem like the keys to solving all problems, she brought a welcome corrective. However, by eschewing the possibility that the miracle of healing could be aided through medicine and surgery, she seemed, to many, to limit the channels through which the power of God could flow.

To the extent that she reminded the world that the healing of the soul is the foremost health goal, Mrs. Eddy was faithful to those New Testament Scriptures she loved so well.

ᛒ

Imagine parents discovering that their nineteen-month-old child has been rendered totally blind and deaf by a mysterious fever. If they, in the midst of their feelings of devastation, could be offered fulfillment of one wish, one prayer answered, surely they would ask for a miracle to restore those missing capacities to their infant. But no physical improvement ever comes.

This is probably just how it was with Arthur and Kate Keller and their daughter, Helen, in 1882. The next chapter in Helen's life is well-known to us, thanks to a popular stage play. A young Irish woman named Annie Sullivan became Helen's teacher (and was known only as "Teacher" through all the years of their relationship). Through persistence and devotion Teacher helped to tame the wild spirit of this frustrated child, to heal her and to evoke the great intelligence and sensitivity within.

It was Teacher who was honored in the title role of *The Miracle Worker*. The miracle was not a cure; it was a healing. Helen was made whole. In one of her many published books, *My Religion*, Helen Keller made this thought-provoking observation: "I cannot imagine myself without religion. To one who is deaf and blind, the spiritual world offers no difficulty."

The ashes of Helen Keller lie close by those of Annie Sullivan in the crypt of the National Cathedral in Washington, D.C.

ᛒ

A similar, though presumably less traumatic, affliction was experienced by St. Paul. He prayed fervently that God remove the thorn from his flesh. Scholars are uncertain what his affliction was. Did the Apostle have epilepsy? or a disfigurement? or the shingles? Or did he have a powerful craving for something unattainable or immoral? We don't know. We gather that the symptoms were not cured. We do know that Paul became one of the most enthusiastic, fearless, and productive servants of Christ in all history.

Did Paul achieve greatness *in spite of* or *because of* his malady? Again we don't know. But perhaps there is a clue in Thornton Wilder's *The Angel That Troubled the Waters*. In response to a person seeking cure for an affliction of the soul the angel says:

"Without your wound, where would your power be? It is your remorse that makes your low voice tremble in the hearts of men. The very angels themselves cannot persuade the wretched and blundering children of the earth as can one human being broken on the wheels of living."

AIDS Memorial in Medicine Bay   Mary Bloom

The distinction between curing and healing is well-understood by the members of Alcoholics Anonymous. They accept the fact that they are alcoholics and always will be. One of their chief assertions is that there is no cure for alcoholism. But then, through simple yet profound practices and affirmations, they attempt with God's help to heal one another of the sickness of the soul which triggered the craving for artificial escape. The primary support comes not from clinics or wonder drugs or sage writings; it comes from others who have suffered.

And in the deepest sense the power of the Cross derives from the belief that God has suffered as one of us. Jesus could have escaped, and obviously the thought entered his mind when he prayed at the Mount of Olives, "Father, if it be thy will, take this cup away from me." But then immediately followed the larger prayer: "Yet not my will but thine be done."

To avoid the ultimate confrontation with human evil would have been a cure; it would have removed his exposure to killing pain. But by submitting to God's will, he remained healed and became a source of healing for his followers through the ages.

The Religious Life Bay

The sixth bay on the right (south) side of the nave honors religious life and focuses on the foremost monk (St. Benedict) and the foremost friar (St. Francis) in Western Christianity.

In **the rosette,** 1 St. Benedict, founder of Christendom's major monastic group and history's first abbot, holds an open book on which are the Latin words with which his Benedictine Rule begins: *Ausculti O Fili Praecepta Magis* (*Harken, O son, to the precepts of the master*). He is attended by St. Dominic (founder of the Dominicans) and St. Clare (foundress of the Poor Clares, patterned after the order of her friend and hero, St. Francis).

In **the cusps,** or petals, are six female figures symbolizing the vows and obligations of monastic life: Poverty, Chastity, Obedience, Labor, Mercy, and Charity. The triangular traceries present the symbols of 2 the premier monk, St. Benedict, on the left and 3 the premier friar, St. Francis, on the right.

The major diamonds in the left lancet present scenes of the life and influence of St. Benedict (480–550 C.E.) and should be read from the bottom to the top: 4 the cave at Subiaco to which Benedict first retreated; 5 one monk tilling the soil while another writes a manuscript, depicting labor, a monastic obligation; 6 worship, the deepest shared experience, represented by the Latin *Opus Dei* (the work of God); 7 St. Benedict's vision of his sister, Scholastica, who became the first Benedictine nun.

The minor medallions: 8 John the Baptist, who emerged from a life of asceticism and denial to preach repentance and the coming of Christ; 9 St. Augustine of Hippo, who formed a quasimonastic order in between his riotous youth and his emergence as priest, bishop of Hippo, and major Christian writer; 10 St. Anthony of Egypt, one of the Desert Fathers and at 105 the longest-lived of the saints; 11 St. Pachomius, another Desert Father and the founder of

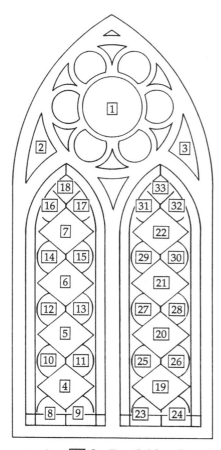

early monasteries; 12 St. Basil (the Great), early monastic leader and an inspiration to St. Benedict; 13 the Cluniacs, whose abbey was the largest in the Middle Ages, cited as St. Gregory VII honors St. Hugh of Cluny; 14 the Cistercians, represented by St. Bernard's vision of the Virgin Mary; 15 the Carthusian Bruno, abbot and later saint, receives young men into his order; 16 St. Norbert, founder of the Premonstratensians (Norbertines), having a vision in a deserted chapel; 17 St. Robert, founder of the Cistercian order, establishing Citeaux. At the peak of the lancet is 18 St. Clare, mentioned in 1 ,the rosette description.

The major diamonds in the right lancet, reading bottom to top, present chronological glimpses of the life of St. Francis of Assisi (1181–1226): 19 St. Francis renounces his inheritance; 20 St. Francis espouses poverty, chastity, and obedience; 21 St. Francis preaches to the birds; 22 St. Francis receives the stigmata (scars on his hands corresponding with those suffered by Jesus at the Crucifixion), signifying his selflessness and spiritual harmony with Jesus Christ.

The minor medallions of the right lancet start with scenes of Francis's early life: 23 St. Francis carousing; 24 St. Francis hearing the words "Repair my church" and being converted; 25 St. Dominic (1170–1221) having a vision of St. Peter and St. Paul urging him to preach; 26 St. Clare repelling the attacking Saracens at Assisi by producing a monstrance (the instrument used to display the sacrament); 27 St. Ignatius Loyola, founder of the Society of Jesus (Jesuits), pictured in his all-night vigil at the Chapel of Our Lady at Montserrat, Spain; 28 one of the Sisters of Charity in cornette ministering to the sick.

The last five are Anglicans: 29 Father Richard Mieux Benson, founder of the Society of St. John the Evangelist, dispatching a missionary to India; 30 Father Huntington, founder of the Order of the Holy Cross, blessing a priest headed for Liberia; 31 John Mason Neale, founder of the Society of St. Margaret, receiving an orphan; 32 a teaching sister of the Community of St. Mary (founded 1865) with children; 33 at the peak of the lancet, the mother foundress of the Community of the Transfiguration with a child.

 *Commentary*

The Yearning to Be Wholly Holy

We glimpse of them on rare occasions, more likely on the screen than in real life: gentle folks in hooded robes of black, brown, or white. These are monks, friars, or contemplative nuns, people who have chosen for their own sake — and the sake of the world — to dwell apart from society's mainstream, united in worship, self-denial, and work. Removal from constant exposure to secularism and materialism seems to many of them the best path toward becoming wholly holy.

The roots of religious life are numerous and ancient. Elijah withdrew from society to purify himself before inveighing against a profane world. John the Baptist did likewise. There are monks (as distinct from priests) in Taoism, Hinduism, and Buddhism. Even aggressive Islam has its marabouts, whose lives are marked by devotion, abnegation, and separation from the secular world.

In its earliest days the Christian fellowship was purified by persecution. Only those who were totally committed, who believed the Beatitudes, lived by the meaning of the Crucifixion, and rejoiced in the Resurrection, would risk death by professing their acceptance of Jesus Christ. But as Christianity gained acceptance in the Roman empire, this purity became diluted. It was then that monastic groups formed around the Desert Fathers: Augustine of Hippo, Anthony of Egypt, Pachomius, and Basil of Caesarea.

It was from Rome itself that the greatest of all monastic leaders, Benedict, retreated — first to a cave at Subiaco, then to the highlands of Mount Cassino. The first abbot in Christendom, Benedict set forth the rules — organizational and spiritual — that remain the basic standards for Western religious life.

Like the broad Christian fellowship from which it had withdrawn, the monastery movement was noblest when poor or under siege and most vulnerable when it met success. Monks who took the personal vow of poverty grew to be among the wealthiest groups and largest land owners in Western Europe.

Reforms were instituted, often resulting in new, more stringent orders. Bernard of Clairvaux was a highly vocal reformer. But railing against sin is never as winsome as making virtue attractive. That was the achievement of St. Francis of Assisi, perhaps the most beloved Christian since New Testament times. The prototype friar, Francis begged and shared and laughed and sang and forbad his fellow mendicants from accumulating any material possessions. The nudity of Francis was more appealing than the hair shirt of Bernard; and to this day there are more Franciscans than members of any other order.

So what about these hooded, robed brothers and sisters of ours? Are they relevant in an age of electronics, space probes, miracle drugs, and computers? Only if the purpose of life, the meaning of death, the nature of our Creator, our alienation from and our reconciliation with that Creator are relevant. The answer is in the soul of the beholder.

The Armed Forces Bay

The easternmost bay on the south aisle honors those who have defended their homelands in battle, especially those who made the supreme sacrifice. It is dedicated to two saints who are wrapped in legend: St. Michael and St. George. St. Michael, the Archangel, is mentioned in the biblical books of Daniel and Revelation, writings laden with symbolic myth. St. George is the patron of Venice, Genoa, Portugal, Greece, and England. The last designation came after he reportedly appeared to Richard Coeur de Lion during the Crusades and inspired the victory at Antioch. His dates are unknown and his historical existence is widely debated.

1 **The rosette** at the top of the arcade window depicts St. George and the dragon. The six surrounding cusps represent major battles engaged in by the 1st Division of the U.S. Expeditionary Forces during World War I. 2 The left tracery triangle commemorates the 4,204 members of that division who were killed; 3 the right triangle honors the 19,141 who were injured. 4 The center triangle shows the number "1" for the first division.

The major medallions of the left lancet feature military events and heroes. They are to be read from the bottom: 5 Constantine's vision before the Battle of Milvian Bridge, 312 C.E.; 6 the Battle of Tours fought by Charles Martel, 732 C.E.; 7 George Washington at Valley Forge at Christmas time, 1777; 8 the surrender of Burgoyne at the Battle of Saratoga, 1777.

The minor medallions of the left lancet continue the military theme: 9 St. Cornelius, third-century pope and martyr; 10 St. Alban, the first English martyr; 11 Charles Martel (grandfather of Charlemagne), who won the Battle of Tours; 12 George Washington; 13 Ulysses S. Grant; and 14 Robert E. Lee.

The main medallions of the right lancet feature naval events and heroes: 15 the Battle of Lepanto, 1571; 16 the defeat of the Spanish Armada, 1588. 17 the Battle of Trafalgar, 1805. 18 the fight between the *Constitution* and *Guerrière* (1812).

The minor medallions of the right lancet continue the naval theme: 19 Sir Francis Drake (1543–96), premier British seafarer; 20 John Paul Jones (1747–92), Scottish-born naval officer in the American Revolution; 21 Admiral George Dewey (1837–1917), U.S. naval officer who defeated the Spanish fleet at Manila Bay; 22 Admiral David Farragut (1801–70); 23 David Henderson (1840–1906), veterans' rights advocate; 24 Commander William Sims (1858–1936), who had a major influence on U.S. ship design and fleet tactics.

The four quarter circles at the base of the two lancets show figures representing 25 the Army, 26 the Air Force, 27 the Navy, and 28 the Marines.

The window was made by Ernest W. Lakeman.

 *Commentary*

War and Peace

Few issues divide thoughtful, moral people more than confrontation and nonviolence. Should we never offer physical resistance? Is nothing worth fighting for?

Jesus advised us to turn the other cheek. Perhaps he was presupposing a context in which the turning of the other cheek would have meaning. Does one turn the other cheek to a tiger in the primeval jungle or to an addict in the human jungle? And what about the plight of others? Are we forbidden intervention on behalf of oppressed races or enslaved nations?

Honest differences of outlook have been expressed from this Cathedral pulpit. An eminent speaker (Kurt Vonnegut) declared, "The only reason World War II was called a 'good war' was that there were no television cameras to record the bloodshed and brutality." But an equally thoughtful preacher (Canon Edward Nason West) affirmed, "The only reason that World War II didn't start *sooner* was that there was no video transmission from Auschwitz and Buchenwald." Both of them may have been right. Perhaps all wars are bad, but some are unavoidable, given the evils that have preceded them.

The never-ending tension between pacifism and *realpolitik* was keenly felt in the 1991 war in the Persian Gulf. A thoughtful analysis of this form of tension had been made by the controversial Henry Kissinger in accepting the 1973 Nobel peace award:

Armed Forces Bay: St. George slays dragon

"Throughout history there have been two approaches to politics: that of the Prophet and that of the Statesman. The Prophet believes in the absoluteness of pure truth, and he recognizes no obstacles in its way.... The Statesman can only learn from history of the contingency of human aspirations, of the possibility of tragedy and the potentiality of failure. Most great transformations have been achieved by the Prophets and it is quite possible that the Statesmen ... set their sights too low and bring on what they seek to avoid. But it is possible that the Prophets in their quest for purity have brought about even greater suffering."

Armed Forces Bay: General George Washington at Valley Forge

Whereas the Christian church hates sin, it loves sinners. It therefore reaches out to all who sincerely attempt to do God's will regardless of their differences of viewpoint: the prophet, the statesman, the soldier, the pacifist. Without abdicating a sense of right and wrong, the designers of this Cathedral felt that those who risked (and often lost) their lives defending the freedom of others should be remembered by those whom they attempted to benefit.

The Armed Forces window presents a few such heroes, particularly from American history. The fact that Robert E. Lee appears on a par with Ulysess S. Grant is not a statement in favor of secession. Much less is it an endorsement of slavery. It is simply an acknowledgement of a great American warrior who selflessly pursued what he believed to be right and did so with dedication and nobility.

Because our Cathedral has two huge transepts yet to be built, it is possible that there will yet be a window celebrating those who have striven for peace and justice through nonviolent strategies: Mahatma Gandhi, Martin Luther King, Jr., Olaf Palme, Dag Hammerskjold, Archbishop Desmond Tutu.

The Nave Clerestory Windows

North Aisle

At the top of the north and south walls of the nave are sixteen large clerestory windows, eight on each side. Each window is forty-five feet in height. The major figure in each of the long lancets is more than twelve feet high.

For the most part, the iconography of each clerestory window presents the same theme as the arcade window beneath it. However, no clerestory window can be studied from the same spot as its corresponding arcade window. Hence the clerestories are presented as a group and not as part of their respective bays.

Sports Clerestory

The first window on the north side highlights sports and physical discipline. As discussed under "Good Sports," p. 44, the theme combines two seemingly contradictory experiences: recreation (play) and discipline. However, exercising and conditioning are prerequisite to good performance in sports; they are likewise essential to maintaining a proper temple for the soul.

1 The symbol of Christ on the Cross is so powerful that we may overlook the stamina, endurance, and courage demonstrated by our Lord. A strange crown for sports, perhaps, but a transcendent instance of physical discipline. This particular form of Crucifix is called "Christ, the Tamer of Wild Horses."

2 Nimrod was described as "a mighty hunter before the Lord" (Gen. 10:8–9). Wild animals were a danger to life and property, so Nimrod was a protector rather than a fox-and-hounds sportsman.

3 The predella portrays threatening animals: fox, wildcat, snake, shark, tiger, and crocodile.

4 The right lancet presents St. Hubert. (See p. 43 for a biographical sketch.)

5 The predella, with the stag to the left, shows St. Hubert's conversion, with the Crucifix appearing between the stag's antlers.

Made by Willet Studios of Philadelphia, this window is the gift of Colonel Robert Pentland.

Arts Clerestory

The second window to the north (left) celebrates arts, crafts, and beauty. It is the work of Charles J. Connick and was given by Lillian Sefton Thomas Dodge in memory of Vincent Benjamin Thomas.

1 Christ is attended by angels with flaming wings. One holds lilies of the field, symbolic of natural beauty. Another presents a model of the Cathedral of St. John the Divine, symbolizing the human effort to create beauty to the glory of God. A rainbow encircles all.

2 St. Cecilia (Cecily), third-century martyr and patron of music, is surrounded by choirs of birds and angels. A pipe organ, of which legend has her the inventor, is also shown.

3 Moses sings his hymns of praise (Exod. 15:1–18) celebrating the deliverance of the Israelites from Pharaoh's army.

Crusaders'

Education

2 The left tracery: the Maltese Cross (four intersecting arrows), the signum of the Knights of St. John of Jerusalem.

3 The right tracery: the Lion of Richard Coeur-de-Lion.

4 Godfrey de Bouillon, one of the few leaders of the Crusades who were both noble and triumphant.

5 A Crusader on horseback.

6 Richard Coeur-de-Lion, sixth king of England, a Crusader who was highly romanticized by troubadours and Robin Hood.

7 A kneeling knight supports the coat of arms of Richard.

Education Clerestory

The fourth window on the north (the left side as one faces the altar) features education. The work of Millet Studios in Philadelphia, it is the gift of Mary Louise Moffatt.

1 As in the Education Bay rosette below, the clerestory rosette presents the twelve-year-old Jesus among the doctors and teachers of the Temple. Here *he* is questioning *them*.

2 St. Hilda (614–80), abbess of Whitby and convenor of its famous synod, is shown in Benedictine habit. The staff and book signify her role as a zealous educator and shepherd of her students. The latter are represented by small heads above her.

3 Another British educator, John Colet, dean of Old St. Paul's Cathedral and lecturer at Oxford, is shown in the predella.

4 St. Thomas Aquinas (1225–74), theologian, teacher, doctor of the church, and author of the influential *Summa Theologica,* is shown in his Dominican scholar's cap with a book and pen. His traditional emblem, a flaming sun with a divine eye in the center, is also presented.

5 Bishop Fulbert who, like St. Thomas, promoted education in France, holds an open book with the monogram of the Virgin Mary. This depicts his devotion to Our Lady of Chartres and its outstanding medieval school.

4 St. Dunstan, the patron of artists and artisans and archbishop of Canterbury, is shown in vestments and holding a pastoral staff. The hammer and the chime of bells represent his manual and artistic skills.

5 The Virgin Mary sings her song of praise (The Magnificat) at the home of her cousin, St. Elizabeth (Luke 1:46–55).

Crusaders' Clerestory

The third window on the north honors the Crusaders. (See "The Crusaders' Bay," pp. 48–49, for further commentary on this controversial chapter in Christian history.) The window was made by Ernest W. Lakeman.

1 The rosette: the seated Christ as the Lion of Judah, as described by St. John the Divine in Revelation 5:5. In his right hand is the scepter; his left hand holds the Book.

Law Clerestory

The fifth window on the left highlights the origins of Jewish and Christian Law. It is the work of Wilbur Herbert Burnham, a memorial given by the children of Charles and Elizabeth Stillman.

1 The glorified Christ, seated and wearing a crown, is portrayed as the Lawgiver. He holds an open book in his left hand and uses his right to emphasize the Law. The tracery triangles show the eternal fountain and the burning bush, among the many symbols of the Virgin Mary. They suggest the mercy with which justice must be tempered.

2 St. Paul, who helped to promote the New Law (New Testament), is shown with a sword and an open book. The sword evokes his militant imagery ("the whole armor of God," Eph. 6:11) The book reminds us that his letters to churches and individuals comprise the greatest number of biblical books (thirteen) to come from the hand of any single contributor.

3 Paul is brought before Herod Agrippa, Palestinian king (Acts 25:13–26:32).

4 Moses holds the Law (Ten Commandments), which he received on Mount Sinai (Exod. 20:1–17).

5 Angered when he finds his fellow Israelites worshiping a golden calf, Moses hurls the tablets to the ground (Exod. 32:15–20).

Anglican History Clerestory

The sixth window on the north (left) side highlights two of the major figures in the formation of the Church of England: the Celtic and the papal (Roman) sources. Made by Wilbur Herbert Burnham, it was given in memory of David Palmer, Mary Katharine Palmer, and Susan Flanders Palmer by Edgar Palmer.

1 Above all, in the rosette, is the glorified Christ with a crown on his head. He is seated upon a dais and holds the scepter and orb of sovereignty. This depiction is called *Panto crator*, ruler of the world. The Alpha and Omega (Rev. 1:18) in gold are woven into the background.

2 St. Augustine (died 604) is portrayed in the rich vestments of archbishop. Dispatched from Rome in 596 by Pope Gregory the Great to Christianize England, he became the first archbishop of Canterbury.

3 The predella shows Augustine baptizing Ethelbert, king of Kent.

4 St. Aidan (died 651) has a miter on his head, a pastoral staff in his right hand, and a book embellished with a golden cross in his left hand. Irish-born,

Law

Anglican History

Aidan went to Iona off the Scottish coast. He was supportive of King Oswald, who later gave him Lindisfarne (Holy Island), where he became its first bishop.

5 In the predella, King Oswald, who himself was later canonized, receives St. Aidan's blessing.

Historical Clerestory

Located above the last bay on the north (left) side, the Historical Clerestory is the only one in which Christ does not appear. Made by Ernest W. Lakeman, the window was given in memory of John Jacob Astor.

1 The rosette features Judas Maccabeus, a Judean in the second century B.C.E., who rose from the ranks of guerrilla fighter to commander in the rebellion against the Syrians. The Jews had been oppressed by the Syrians and had seen pagan worship instituted in Jerusalem. Judas's small, dedicated force, although outnumbered, were able to liberate the great city. They destroyed heathen idols and rebuilt the Temple. Those triumphs, commemorated in the Jewish feast of Hanukkah, are recorded in the First Book of Maccabees of the Apocrypha. Judas Maccabeus is

Historical

Fatherhood

shown at prayer while an angel with a flaming sword disperses the enemy.

2 St. Alban, Roman soldier and first British martyr (third century C.E.) appears in armor holding a palm branch (symbol of ultimate victory).

3 The predella shows Alban being sentenced by the Roman governor.

4 The Venerable Bede (673–735) wrote the *Ecclesiastical History of England*, our major source of knowledge of Christian England in the earliest centuries. A popular figure during his lifetime and thereafter, he was proclaimed a doctor of the church in 1899.

5 Bede's deathbed scene is portrayed in the predella. He is reported to have dictated and prayed until his dying breath.

Fatherhood Clerestory

At the eastern end of the north aisle, above the door leading to the stoneyard, is the Fatherhood window, designed and made by Willet Studios. It is given in memory of George Forrest Butterworth, one-time chancellor of the Diocese of New York.

1 Christ and St. Philip are shown at the moment when the latter has said, "Lord, show us the Father and we shall be satisfied." Jesus replied, "He who has seen me has seen the Father" (John 14:8–9).

2 Abraham with his sons Isaac and Ishmael occupies the left lancet. On Abraham's chest is the star of David; Ishmael is dark skinned and holds the crescent and star of Islam; next to him is Isaac holding a cross. Above, the hand of God is inserting the letters "HA" into the name "ABRAM," making it "ABRAHAM," "Father of Many Nations" (Gen. 17:4–5)

3 David grieves as his rebellious son, Absalom, is caught by his long hair in tree branches and slain by Joab (2 Sam. 18:1–17).

4 The Holy Family is presented with St. Joseph as protector of the Mother and Child. At the apex of the lancet is a budding staff (Joseph's emblem) superimposed on a carpenter's square.

5 A forgiving father welcomes the prodigal son home while the elder brother works in the field beside the fatted calf.

Far beneath the window, at eye level, is a plaque to Irving Bloomingdale, famous New York merchant and a contributor to the construction of the Cathedral.

Cleaning a portion of the half acre of stained-glass   Mary Bloom

The Nave Clerestory Windows

South Aisle

All Souls' Clerestory

The first clerestory window on the right, or south, side of the nave was designed and made by the firm of Heinigke and Smith. It was the gift of the alumnae of the School of Nursing at St. Luke's Hospital. Its style is consistent with directives of the Second Council of Nicea in the eighth century and reflects the iconography that is still dominant in the Eastern Orthodox Church.

1 The rosette reveals Christ delivering imprisoned souls. Prime among them is Adam, whose halo is being restored. In the tracery slots are 2 the mythical phoenix, which rises newborn from its own ashes (a Greek symbol adapted by Christianity to symbolize the Resurrection), and 3 the peacock who sheds feathers only to grow new ones even more brilliant (another Resurrection symbol popular in the Middle Ages).

4 The valley of dry bones (Ezek. 37:1–14) from the prophet's vision is presented. Ezekiel himself appears at the bottom holding a quill with which to record the vision. The four winds, with which God breathed flesh and life back into those bones, are shown in the corners. This is seen as a prefiguration of the Resurrection.

5 In the predella Christ is shown receiving the Virgin Mary's soul into heaven.

6 Christ in glory emerges from the tomb bearing the banner of victory. At the bottom is a small figure of Saul (later called Paul) experiencing conversion on the road to Damascus.

7 A priest celebrates the Holy Communion surrounded by the unseen congregation at the point of the words, "therefore, with Angels and Archangels and with all the company of heaven, we laud and magnify thy glorious name."

All Souls'

Missionary

Missionary Clerestory

The second window on the right side of the nave was made by Willet Studios of Philadelphia and given in memory of Philip Newbold Rhinelander and Newbold Rhinelander Landon.

1 The rosette offers a Byzantine representation of the Virgin Mary with the Greek word *Theotokos* (God bearer) written above her head. In front of her, shown as an adult/child, is Jesus Christ with the Greek abbreviations of his name and title: IC XC.

2 Isaiah, one of the four major prophets, is shown wearing a prayer shawl and holding a two-handled saw, the legendary instrument of his martyrdom.

3 The prophet's vision (Isa. 6:1–9) is recalled by the six-winged seraph and the purifying hot coal.

4 St. Peter is identified by the inverted cross (on which he is reported to have died), keys entwined with a streamer marked *Petros*, and the stone beneath his foot inscribed *Petra*. Surely the most far-reaching pun in history was Christ's statement "You are Peter [*petros*] and on this rock [*petra*] will I build my church" (Matt. 16:13–19).

Labor   Communications

 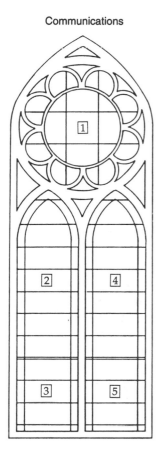

5 Three people of three different races recall Peter's vision and response (Acts 10:9–42). The interpretation is that God's church is for all people.

Labor Clerestory

The third of the highest windows on the right (south) side of the nave was created by Nicola D'Ascenzo. The sacredness of work in the building and preserving of the world is the theme.

1 Christ is shown in the Garden of Eden, standing on the Tree of Life and giving the first man and woman implements for their livelihood. Adam receives a shovel; Eve a distaff (cleft branch) for use in spinning.

2 Joseph the patriarch is shown with a scepter (signifying his rise to power in Egypt) and waters (suggesting the Nile River).

3 Emblems of Joseph's dreams, aspirations, and accomplishments are wheat, a cow, sun, moon, stars, and a rainbow.

4 The New Testament Joseph holds the tools of his craft, the square and compass. The lion at his feet denotes his descent from King David of the tribe of Judah.

5 An angel bears a yoke from which are suspended the Cross and the fleur-de-lis (the latter a symbol of the Virgin Mary). These emblems honor the burden accepted by Joseph as guardian of the Holy Family.

Communications Clerestory

Another window by Nicola D'Ascenzo, the fourth high window on the south side of the nave, was given in memory of James Muhlenberg Bailey by Alleta R. Bailey.

1 The figure of Christ seated on a rainbow is known as *The Majestas*. It represents Christ as fulfillment of Isaiah's prophecy, "He shall judge among the nations" (Isa. 2:4). The tri-radiant nimbus (halo) is used exclusively to denote one of the persons of the Holy Trinity. The geometric figure surrounding *The Majestas* is called a "mandorla" or "vesica" and is reserved solely for identifying Christ or the Virgin Mother in glory.

The writers of the first two Gospels are featured in the two lancets. This is meant to proclaim that the "good news" of the Gospels is the basis of all saving communication.

2 St. Matthew's symbols are a scroll (Gospel writer) and a purse (tax collector).

3 The predella shows Matthew being called to serve as a disciple.

4 St. Mark's contribution (the earliest Gospel) is represented by the book in his hand.

5 St. Mark and St. Timothy hurry to take books and parchments to St. Paul at Troas.

Medical Clerestory

The fifth high window on the south side of the nave was made by Reynolds, Francis, and Rohnstock. It memorializes the de Peyster family, whose presence in America extends back to 1645.

[1] The rosette shows Christ seated at a table, breaking bread and giving it to his disciples. Leftmost is St. Peter, holding a cup. St. John, in the center, is receiving the Eucharist; and to the right is his brother, St. James, holding the bread. The snake represents the brass serpent made by Moses and used by him to heal the sick. It has long been part of the medical emblem.

[2] St. Luke, the Beloved Physician and patron of medicine, holds a closed book and pen denoting his major contribution to the Bible. As author of a Gospel account plus the Acts of the Apostles, he is the most prolific writer of Christian Scripture.

[3] St. Luke, writing his Gospel, is attended by the winged ox, which is his symbol.

[4] Hippocrates (460–400 B.C.E.), Greek physician, although outside of the Judaeo-Christian tradition, represents the universality of God's healing love.

[5] Hippocrates heals a sick man.

Religious Life Clerestory

The sixth of the top windows on the south of the nave, like the adjoining Medical Clerestory, was made by Reynolds, Francis, and Rohnstock.

[1] Christ, espoused to the church, sits enthroned. To his right is a female figure representing the church, often referred to as "the Bride of Christ." To his left, almost in caricature, is a blindfolded female with broken staff and crown askew. She represents the world without Christ.

[2] St. Benedict (480–550), the father of Western monasticism, is portrayed with staff and crown. (See "The Religious Life Bay," pp. 72–73, for further references to St. Benedict).

[3] St. Benedict's successful resistance to sexual temptation is portrayed in the predella as he rebuffs a woman with a wolf's head. (Female wolves were medieval symbols of prostitution.)

[4] Basil (329–80), the father of Eastern monasticism and an inspiration to St. Benedict, is shown with an Eastern crown.

[5] The predella portrays the moment when the youthful Basil miraculously escaped banishment by Emperor Valens, a follower of the Arian heresy.

Medical   Religious Life

Armed Forces Clerestory

Located above the last nave bay on the right (south) side is the window given by General Cornelius Vanderbilt and by Catherine Moulton and her daughter, May T. Hanrahan, in memory and honor of armed forces, European and American, in World War I. This is another of the windows by Ernest W. Lakeman.

[1] Christ is shown as the Prince of Peace. [2] The Cross and [3] the Crown in the tracery triangles affirm that true victory is won by taking up the Cross.

[4] The main figure in the left lancet is St. George, an obscure third-century centurion to whom much legend has accrued. In 1222 he became the patron saint of England after his reported appearance to the forces of Richard during the Crusades. The symbols of the British Armed Forces are over his head and in the border are the coats of arms of the British Commonwealth nations.

[5] Dominating the right lancet is St. Michael, one of the seven archangels. Tradition has him defeating Lucifer after that fallen angel had revolted against God. Michael is often depicted as the personification of Goodness in its ultimate triumph. (See the Peace Fountain in the Cathedral close, p. 150.)

Armed Forces

Motherhood

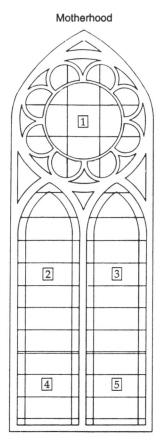

The 43-foot Sports Clerestory window

In the predellas are ⑥ St. Louis and St. Joan of Arc, noble warriors of France; and ⑦ Daniel, delivered from the lions who sit peacefully at the left. The message is that deep faith in God is the ultimate protection against raw, threatening power, echoing the theme of the tracery symbols above.

Motherhood Clerestory

At the eastern end of the south side of the nave, above an exit door, is the Motherhood window, designed by D'Ascenzo of Philadelphia. It was given in memory of Mrs. Hamilton Fairfax, first chair of the Women's Division of the Building Committee of the Cathedral.

① The Virgin Mary and the Child Jesus occupy the rosette. St. Mary's lily is the symbol of purity. The book held by Jesus symbolizes the Word made flesh.

② The left lancet portrays Hannah, her son, Samuel, and the priest, Eli, whose prayers of intercession had helped her produce the child despite her advanced age. The grateful song of Hannah (1 Sam. 1:10) was apparently the model for St. Mary's Magnificat (Luke 2:46–55).

③ St. Helena is shown with the True Cross, which she is reported to have found in Jerusalem, and her son Constantine, whose ascendency to Roman emperor ended the persecution of Christians. At the peak of the lancet is the Cross that Constantine saw in a vision.

The predellas show ④ George Washington kneeling beside his mother and ⑤ Abraham Lincoln kneeling beside his mother.

Beneath the window, just above eye level, is a plaque commemorating the visit of the Queen Mother of England, who dedicated this window on October 31, 1954.

The Rose Windows

great artist, asked to demonstrate his genius, seized a paint brush and drew a circle — not an icosahedron, not a sunset, not a brilliant abstraction, just a circle.

Simplest yet most profound of figures, the circle has in various cultures been invested with metaphysical qualities and significance — particularly in the East. The oriental prayer wheel not only speeds up orisons; it depicts a cyclical concept of life. The wheel of fortune, in existence long before roulette, represents fate, usually in cruel, inexorable form, as in the Hindu juggernaut. The mandala, a circular representation of the universe, is another image from India.

With no beginning and no end, the circle became a symbol for eternity long ago. Its formula root, pi (Greek π), has no discovered resolution or recurrent pattern as its digits march rightward to infinity.

It was perhaps inevitable that Christianity would take this mystical, fateful, endless figure and give it new use and meaning. Prior to the twelfth century small round apertures had appeared in some churches in addition to the narrow window slits. There were oculi and peepholes through which outsiders might observe worship. However, the rebuilding of the abbey church of St. Denis (dedicated 1144) brought a quantum leap forward and upward. Its rose windows were the crowning jewels in a series of daring innovations (pointed arches, ribbed vaulting, and primitive flying buttresses) permitting the church to be bathed in light.

Never mind that within a century windows four times larger would appear elsewhere in France; St. Denis had showed the way. Whether Abbot Suger himself was a major architect in this inspired tour de force, or served primarily as patron and enabler, is not certain. His is the only name we have to thank. His writings reveal a man possessed of deep religious insight and an overpowering determination to let the light of God into the house of God.

Physical illumination became the purveyor of spiritual light. Where the oculus had been empty and the wheel of fortune had portrayed a grinding repetition around its circumference, the rose window focused on the hub. There, highlighted by the spokes and surrounded by richly colored depictions of saints, cherubim, and seraphim, could be found the figure of Christ. The wheel of fate had become a rose of life.

Soon the French Gothic church, in addition to rosettes at the apex of its nave windows, had large rose windows in each transept and at the west end. Further traditions then evolved in which the north rose features St. Mary as the embodiment of all wisdom and virtue preceding Jesus. Surrounding her are the prophets, priests, and kings of the Old Testament. The south rose usually focuses on the Resurrection of Jesus, while the west rose has Christ presiding over the Last Judgment.

An intriguing offshoot of the rose window was the circular labyrinth or maze, laid in stone on some of the church floors in France. Like the Stations of the Cross, the maze invited the worshiper to simulate a pilgrimage. In this case the goal was to reach the center (salvation) without being tempted into a cul-de-sac (sin). Riverside Church in New York has a modest floor labyrinth patterned after the huge mazes at Chartres and Amiens.

Thus have ripples gone forth from Abbot Suger's divine fenestration. Rose windows can be found throughout Christendom and in secular structures as well. Some are purely decorative with no attempt to convey a message. Others deal with a great theme but in abstraction (National Cathedral, Washington, D.C., west). But the first, and arguably the finest, are those in France. It is difficult to imagine a window equal to Chartres, south. To the naked eye it appears as an array of priceless, iridescent gems. Binoculars, however, reveal among them twenty-four human gems of the faith, the martyrs.

The Great Rose Window

The Great Rose Window

Although the meaning, beauty, and setting of a rose window are of paramount importance, size contributes to their impact. Moreover, it indicates the magnitude of structural achievement in cathedrals that were built without hidden metal girders.

Shown below are the diameters claimed for several of Christendom's foremost rose windows. Precise accuracy is not guaranteed; and where the claim seems unusually enthusiastic, a more conservative estimate is also given. In some instances, discrepancies are attributable to differing reference points of measurement: the diameter of the aperture; aperture plus casement; or aperture, casement, plus decorative border. As much as 15 percent variation is thereby possible.

Another variable is the proportion of glass to stone. A thirty-foot diameter does not tell us how much light the rose is admitting. Painton Cowen's classic, *Rose Windows*, makes this point in contrasting the western roses of Chartres and Notre Dame, Paris. In the former, "the whole impression is that the twelve main openings have been punched through a wall," whereas at Paris, "the volume of stone has been pared down to a minimum, leaving a spider's web frame of great strength."

FRANCE	Diameter in feet
Chartres (west)	43–46
Laon (west)	38–45
Notre Dame, Paris (north)	43
Notre Dame, Paris (south)	43
Amiens (north)	37
Chartres (north)	36
Chartres (south)	36
Notre Dame, Paris (west)	33

ENGLAND	
Old St. Paul's (west)	36 *a*
Lancing College (west)	32–36
Westminster Abbey (north)	35
Westminster Abbey (south)	35

UNITED STATES	
St. John the Divine (west)	40
Sacred Heart, Newark (south)	35 *b c*
St. John the Divine (north)	33 *d*
St. John the Divine (south)	33 *d*
Sacred Heart, Newark (east)	32 *b c*
Sacred Heart, Newark (west)	32 *b c*
Blessed Sacrament, New York (north)	32 *e*
St. Patrick's, N.Y. (west)	26 *b*
National Cathedral, Washington, D.C. (west)	26

a destroyed by fire, 1666
b structural metal beams within main stone supports
c main entrance is south; transepts east and west
d not yet constructed
e entrance is at north

As indicated in the chart, the **Great Rose** at St. John's is forty feet in diameter. It contains more than ten thousand pieces of glass. The central figure of Christ seated in glory is 5′ 7″ high. The skeletal stone tracery varies in width from twenty to thirty inches.

In normal reflected light the window is predominantly blue. However a bright western sun kindles the red hues aflame changing the rose into a more natural color.

1 Christ in Glory, 2 Angels and gifts of the spirit, 3 Beatitudes, 4 Evangelist: Matthew, 5 Evangelist: Mark, 6 Evangelist: Luke, 7 Evangelist: John, 8 Prophet: Isaiah, 9 Prophet: Jeremiah, 10 Prophet: Daniel, 11 Prophet: Ezekiel, 12 Divine love: Seraphim, 13 Divine Wisdom: Cherubim

William Woodward gave this window in memory of his parents, William Woodward, Jr., and Sarah Woodward, and his uncle, James T. Woodward. It was designed and executed by Charles J. Connick.

Forming a crescent beneath the Great Rose are the sixty-one state trumpet pipes, one of the strongest organ stops in the world. (See pp. 128–129 for details on the pipe organ.)

The Lesser Rose Window

Beneath the state trumpets and a columned walkway is the **Lesser Rose.** Two roses in one wall are a rarity. Among the world's major cathedrals, Rheims, France, is the only other instance.

Equally rare is a rose with an odd number of divisions. The seven points of this star derive from the Apocalypse of St. John: 14 seven fountains, 15 seven vines, 16 seven pairs of doves, and 17 seven stars. At the window's heart is Our Lord's monogram, the first three letters of "Jesus" (in Greek).

With its twenty-three-foot diameter, the Lesser Rose would dominate most churches. Here it must be subordinate; hence the softened blues and reds and a slightly abstract, mandala-like design. Designed and made by Charles J. Connick, this is the gift of Jane Andrews.

Western Exterior of the Great Rose Window   A. Hansen

The Pilgrims' Pavement

T|he three inner, or main, aisles of the nave were paid for by visitors and pilgrims, many of whom were responding to tours by the Laymen's Club. Known as "The Pilgrims' Pavement," they are paved with slabs of green Vermont argillite, a form of slate, with bands and border of black argillite.

In each of these aisles is a series of medallions. The center disc is, in every case, of black granite with a border of Belgian black marble. Within the larger circles are shields, symbols, and inscriptions in bronze, the details of which are described below.

The center aisle contains the Gospel medallions, depicting events in the earthly life of Jesus Christ. The south aisle features major shrines and saints in Great Britain. The north aisle continues this theme but adds three major shrines in mainland Europe plus special ecclesiastical landmarks in the United States. The center aisle medallions are five and a half feet in diameter; the medallions in the adjacent aisles are a foot smaller.

Center Aisle— Gospel Medallions

[1] *Bethlehem:* A star represents the Nativity; three crowns symbolize the visit of the Magi. The text, from Isaiah: "For unto us a child born, unto us a child is given."

[2] *Nazareth:* The Holy Family is guarded by angels. The fleur-de-lis and the carpenter's square represent St. Mary and St. Joseph respectively. Text: "The child grew and waxed strong in spirit and in wisdom."

[3] *Jordan:* The place of Jesus's baptism is evoked by a lamb ("Lamb of God" was John the Baptist's description of Jesus) and a border of shells. Text: "Thou art my beloved Son; in Thee I am well pleased."

[4] *Cana:* A cup of grapes surrounded with water pots recalls the miracle at the wedding feast. Text: "The beginning of miracles did Jesus in Cana of Galilee."

[5] *Samaria:* A representation of water and a well evoke the words spoken by Jesus to the Samaritan woman. Text: "Whosoever drinketh of the water I shall give shall never thirst."

[6] *Capernaum:* The sun, breaking in on the letters S.P.Q.R. (Senatus Populusque Romanus) depicts the healing of the centurion's servant. Text: "I have not found so great a faith, no not in Israel."

[7] *Mount Tabor:* The Transfiguration is represented by the monogram XP (the first two letters of "Christ" in Greek). The Tables of the Law evoke Moses; the altar, kindled by heavenly fire, stands for Elijah. Text: "This is my beloved Son; hear him."

Bethlehem medallion

A. Leonard Gustafson

[8] *Bethany:* The shrouded figure of Lazarus is being raised from an open tomb. The hand above symbolizes the power of God. Text: "Father, I thank Thee that Thou hast heard Me."

[9] *Bethsaida:* Five barley loaves and two fishes represent the feeding of thousands. Text: "He blessed them and gave to the disciples to set before the multitudes."

[10] Gethsemene, [11] Jerusalem, and [12] Mt. Olivet will be placed in the crossing. The Jerusalem medallion, larger than the others, will be at the heart of the intersection.

North Aisle Medallions

[13] *Westminster:* The five birds are the traditional coat of arms of Edward the Confessor, who founded Westminster Abbey and is buried behind its high altar. The abbey is the coronation church of England and final resting place for many of its most celebrated citizens.

[14] *Gloucester:* Crossed keys represent St. Peter, whose name was taken by this great abbey (now a cathedral) in the west of England.

[15] *Walsingham:* Tradition has this abbey being built in Norfolk, England, at the appearance and behest of St. Mary. Restored in the twentieth century, it remains a pilgrimage goal for many Anglicans and Roman Catholics.

[16] *Cologne:* Above the shield of this West German city are three crowns for the three kings of the Epiphany, who are alleged to be buried in the towering cathedral.

[17] *Compostela:* The traditional tomb of St. James (brother of St. John) has made this Spanish city and its cathedral a popular venue for pilgrims.

[18] *Drake's Bay:* At this point near San Francisco the first Prayer Book service in the Western Hemisphere was held. The stars and waves depict the earth-circling voyage of Britain's Admiral Francis Drake during the sixteenth century.

[19] *Monhegan Island:* The first use of the English Prayer Book in New England took place off the coast of Maine in 1607. Pine trees and waves are the symbols.

[20] *Jamestown:* The royal coat of arms in this medallion represent the first British colony in the New World, Jamestown, Virginia. This was the first place that the English Prayer Book was in steady use.

[21] *Woodbury:* In this Connecticut town (known as "the cradle" of the American episcopate) Samuel Seabury in 1783 became the first elected bishop in America. His coat of arms, plus three castles representing Aberdeen, Scotland (where he was consecrated), form the heraldic device on the medallion.

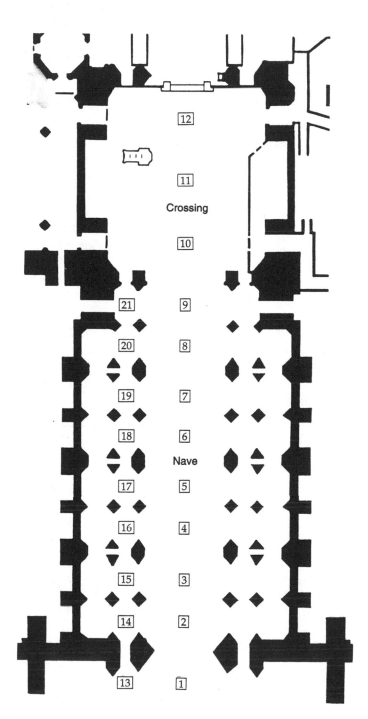

PILGRIMS' PAVEMENT

South Aisle Medallions

22 *Canterbury:* Since 597, Canterbury has been the metropolitan see of all England. Already a pilgrimage goal because of the first archbishop, St. Augustine, the cathedral gained in popularity after a later archbishop, Thomas Becket, was murdered there in 1170 by knights of King Henry II.

23 *Glastonbury:* History and legend have brought great romance to this abbey, now a ruin but once the largest in the land. Joseph of Arimathea is alleged to have brought the chalice (Holy Grail), from which Jesus drank at the Last Supper, to this spot. King Arthur, who, with his knights, searched for the grail, is reported to be buried here.

24 *St. Albans:* This city and cathedral take their name from Britain's protomartyr, who is buried here. A saltire (X-shaped cross) is shown with sword and crown, depicting martyrdom and heavenly reward.

25 *Durham:* The finest Norman church in existence, Durham is beloved because of its patron, St. Cuthbert, and as a border fortress against invaders from the north. A plain cross amid rampaging lions means that faith is the greatest protection against harm.

26 *York:* For centuries this Roman-built city contended with Canterbury for ecclesiastical primacy. The eventual solution was to make York's archbishop primate of England and Canterbury's the primate of *all* England.

27 *St. David's:* David, a sixth-century preacher who became the patron of Wales, moved his see to the southwest tip of Wales, where a city and cathedral bear his name. Five roses symbolize Christ's wounds.

28 *Downpatrick:* This is the burial place of Ireland's patron, St. Patrick. He made many conversions to the faith by using the shamrock (three leaves from one stem) to illustrate the Trinity.

29 *Winchester:* The greatest of English cities in the first millennium, this is the burial city of Wessex kings, including the beloved King Alfred the Great.

30 *St. Andrews:* Long before golf brought fame to this Scottish town, the saint's relics were said to have been placed there. He is Scotland's patron. The fishes on the shield have a double significance. St. Andrew was a fisherman when he was called to follow Jesus. Also it was he who produced the lad with a lunch of rolls and fish, which Jesus used to feed the crowd of five thousand.

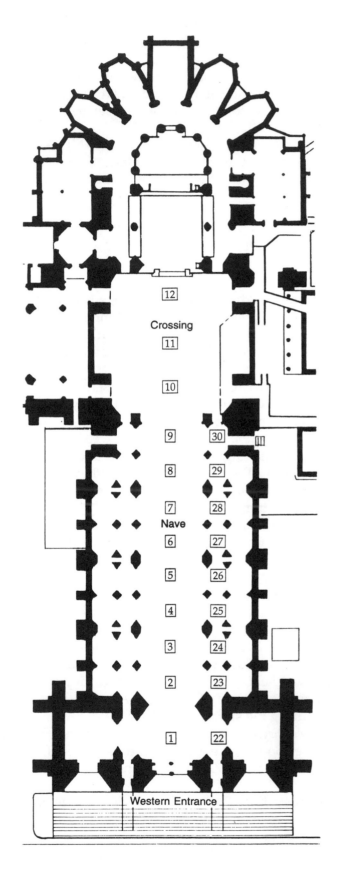

 *Commentary*

Pilgrimage

Most of today's travels are a means to an end, the sole purpose being to get from Point A to Point B. Occasionally the trip will be an end in itself, such as a Sunday drive in the country, in which the only destination, and that deferred, is home.

In a pilgrimage, both the travel and the destination are important. The outbound trip brings purification, preparation, and anticipation, without which the shrine or holy place would not gain its full mystique or make its greatest impact. The pilgrims' readiness and their faith in God's presence and grace contribute to the religious experience at the sacred spot. Then the homeward journey permits them to ponder the feelings and meanings of the whole venture as they take their sense of inspiration and renewal back to workaday life.

The prime motives for pilgrimages have been to give thanks for blessings, to seek healing from affliction, to do penance for sins, and to discharge vows. In addition there is the element of curiosity, the tourists' fascination with famous lives and places.

In the Western world, Jerusalem has held the foremost lure for pilgrims since it has been the prime focus for Christians and Jews and a significant city for Moslems as well. It was the loss of access for Christians to this holy city that triggered the ill-fated Crusades.

As early as the second-century, Rome, with the tombs of St. Peter and St. Paul, was another favorite destination for the devout. Later, Santiago de Compostela in northwestern Spain became the terminus of a network of pilgrim paths leading through the Pyrenees from France. "Santiago" is the Spanish word for St. James; and Compostela's attraction is the tradition that says that James visited there as an Apostle, and that his bones were miraculously brought back to the spot after his martyrdom in Jerusalem. (See the chapter on St. James Chapel, pp. 101–104, for further commentary).

Dating from the murder of Thomas Becket in 1170, Canterbury has been Britain's principal shrine. An Iron Age footpath connecting Winchester with Canterbury thereafter acquired the title "Pilgrim's Way," and was popularized in Hilaire Belloc's *The Old Road*. Another trail, from London to Canterbury, was the setting for Chaucer's *Canterbury Tales*.

Brass rubbing of Bethsaida medallion in pavement of center aisle

Pilgrims traveled with minimal gear. Hence their symbol in religious art is a scrip, or small handbag, symbolizing modest possessions. Often they would purchase emblems of the shrines they had reached and wear them in their hats, a forerunner of automobile bumper stickers. The cockle shell became the symbol of Santiago and can still be seen in walls along that pilgrimage route (see p. 103.)

Other famous shrines, some of which are heavier with legend and lore than with historicity, are:
• Glastonbury, England, where Joseph of Arimathea is alleged to have brought the Holy Grail, where King Arthur and queen Guinevere are said to be buried, and where St. Patrick formed a monastic group. • St. Denis, Paris, where the bones of France's protomartyr repose. • Cologne, Germany, where the bones of the Wise Men are said to be entombed. • Loreto, Italy; Fatima, Portugal; Lourdes, France; and Walsingham, England, all associated with reported appearances of the Virgin Mary.

John Bunyan, in *Pilgrim's Progress*, presents all of life as an urgent pilgrimage toward the Heavenly City. It is fraught with temptations and persecutions and mined with such traps as the Valley of Despair, the Valley of the Shadow of Death, and Vanity Fair. It serves as a corrective to any who might romanticize the physical or spiritual pilgrimage or trivialize its rigors.

The Cathedra (bishop's seat)

Eastern Interior

Capitals of eight granite pillars at east end

Cathedral Archives

The Crossing

ost cathedrals and abbeys are cruciform in design. The long arm from the western entrance to high altar at the east end is intersected by a shorter north/south arm, the extremes of which are the north and south transepts. Among the notable exceptions are the Roman Catholic cathedrals at Palma, Majorca, and Bourges, France, which have no transepts. The Anglican cathedrals at Salisbury, Lincoln, and Liverpool have two sets of transepts each and the Metropolitan Cathedral (Roman Catholic) at Liverpool is built in the round.

Faced with limited space in urban settings, some architects have designed churches that at ground level are basically rectangular in shape but become cruciform as they reach higher levels. This technique was employed at Notre Dame, Paris, and adapted at St. Patrick's in New York. Visitors to the latter church building will note that the transepts appear to be short at the exterior base but lengthy when viewed from within or from the heights of the RKO building.

The area where the two arms of a cruciform church intersect is the "crossing." It is one of the inevitable problems confronting a cathedral architect. And, as already noted (see p. 41), Ralph Adams Cram inherited a challenge unprecedented in Gothic churches. The four huge granite arches had already set the parameters. The innermost area to be accommodated was 100 feet square (10,000 square feet). With the main piers included, the crossing measures at 126 per side (nearly 16,000 square feet). This is four times the crossing area of the National Cathedral in Washington, D.C., three times that of the celebrated octagon at Ely, England, and approximately the same size as the rotundas at the Duomo in Florence and St. Paul's in London (which are not Gothic structures). St. Peter's Basilica in Rome (also non-Gothic) is the only stone church in Christendom with a greater crossing area (18,770 square feet).

A central tower of these dimensions would be disproportionately large, even for such a gigantic church. On the other hand, a fleche or spire might seem trivial as the crowning ornament. Cram's solution was to reduce the sides of the square to 60 feet at the 150-foot level. The result, as seen in the most commonly used model of the completed structure (designed in 1926), composes very well. In any case, a central tower would follow the western towers and the transepts on the construction agenda, which may leave time for future generations to change the Cram plans, even as Cram himself altered those of Heins and LaFarge. One suggestion has been put forth that would call for laser beams projecting upward from the four exterior corners of the crossing to converge at a lofty spot (presumably well above the 528-foot record height of the tower at Ulm Cathedral, Germany).

Changes of taste and outlook may also affect the completion of the interior of the crossing. The tiled dome, constructed by Guastavino, originally planned as a temporary covering until a lantern tower was erected, has won so much attention and acclaim that it may remain in some decorated or illuminated form. Likewise, the massive granite piers and arches were planned to be finished off in limestone. Many now hope that at least part of the granite, symbolizing the strength and permanence of the Rock of Ages, will always remain visible.

At various times the crossing, at floor level, will contain a temporary altar, a small pipe organ, a grand piano, a reading desk, or a thousand chairs. All are free standing and hence portable. However, **the pulpit,** weighing many tons, and **the lectern** are permanent. The pulpit was designed by Henry Vaughan, the architect of three of the apsidal chapels. Since Vaughan was also an architect of the National Cathedral in Washington, D.C., he is the artistic link between the two largest cathedrals in the Western Hemisphere.

The entire pulpit is made of Tennessee marble, an uncrystalline limestone. The newel posts fram-

The Pulpit

[95]

ing the stairs present statues of two great prophets of the Old Dispensation: Isaiah and St. John the Baptist. Girding the pulpit at eye level, reading counterclockwise from the stairs, are scenes from the life of Christ: the Nativity, Jesus and the Doctors in the Temple, the Crucifixion, the Resurrection, and the Supper at Emmaus. In the smaller niches bordering these scenes are figures of eight great Christian preachers: St. Jerome; St. Gregory; St. John Chrysostom; St. Peter; St. Paul; the English bishop and martyr Hugh Latimer (1485–1555); the French bishop Jacques Bossuet (1627–1704); and the American Bishop Phillips Brooks (1835–93).

Beneath these carvings are two horizontal moldings: one is a grape vine, symbolizing Christ the True Vine; the other is of roses representing Christ the Rose of Sharon. At the base are the four Evangelists — St. Matthew, St. Mark, St. Luke, and St. John with their traditional symbols. On the side of the pulpit stairs is inscribed "In memory of Henry Codman Potter, the gift of Mrs. Russell Sage, A.D. 1916." The wrought iron gates on the pulpit were the gift of Mr. and Mrs. George Arents.

Opposite the pulpit, on what is called "the Epistle side," is **the Eagle Lectern**. Made of bronze, the lectern is a replica of an ancient eagle found in a lake near St. Albans Abbey, England. The eagle stands on a globe, around the base of which are the four Evangelists: St. Matthew with an open book; St. Mark with a closed book and a pen; St. Luke with an open book in one hand and a pen in the other; and St. John with a chalice. Their traditional symbols are below. The Eagle Lectern is the gift of Mary Gertrude Edson Aldrich in memory of Bishop Horatio Potter.

When the north and south transepts have been constructed, the concrete wall on the sides of the crossing will be removed and the tapestries relocated. Each transept is designed to have its own rose window thirty-three feet in diameter. The Cathedral will then join Notre Dame, Rheims, in having four rose windows. The distance between the transept roses will be 330 feet, longer than the full length of most of the world's cathedrals. Arcade and clerestory windows will illuminate these transepts, giving future generations a chance to compensate for honors or emphases overlooked by earlier iconographers.

The Aeolian Skinner pipe organ console

The Apse and Ambulatory

To the north, east, and south of the choir and high altar is a portion of the church called the "apse." In most English cathedrals the apse is polygonal, often designed with right angles. In a majority of French cathedrals, the apse curves around the high altar in a semicircle. St. John's follows the French pattern.

In either tradition, the apse consists of a walking area or passageway called the "ambulatory," plus one or more apsidal chapels, radiating outward from it. These chapels are customarily named for saints who, in a concept that emerged in the Middle Ages, are seen as cushioning the head of Christ, represented by the high altar. The French word for apse, *chevet*, also means cushion.

The ambulatory at St. John's is 14 feet wide and approximately 250 feet in total length. The pavement is of clay-red tiles with borders of green serpentine and green Pennsylvania marble. The wainscoting between the great pillars is of Grecian marble from the island of Skyros. The ambulatory presently gives access to seven chapels and the baptistry.

A chapel is an area of worship that is an adjunct to some larger entity. Our thirteen chapels (seven in the apse and six in the nave) are obviously components of the Cathedral. Across 114th Street there is a chapel within St. Luke's Hospital. Across Amsterdam Avenue and up three blocks is St. Paul's Chapel of Columbia University. Many famous castles and palaces of the Western world likewise have chapels: Versailles in France, Windsor Castle in England, Escorial in Spain.

Virtually every cathedral has at least one chapel. Some chapels, such as those in the apse at St. John's, are almost separate structures with three walls and a roof of their own. Others may be clustered indentations in an outer wall of the main church structure. Many of the record number of fifty-nine chapels at the National Shrine of the Immaculate Conception in Washington, D.C., have been constructed in that latter fashion.

All Roman Catholic cathedrals and many Anglican cathedrals have a Lady Chapel, dedicated to the Blessed Virgin Mary. The Lady Chapel is invariably the most resplendent and frequently the easternmost of the apsidal chapels. Although St. John's does not have a Lady Chapel, the entire north transept has been dedicated to the Blessed Virgin Mary and will contain its own altar.

Consistent with the dominant theme and imagery at St. John's, the apsidal chapels were designed with the Revelation of St. John in mind and are called the "Chapels of the Tongues." The word "tongues" in the Book of Revelation means languages or nationalities. Revelation 7:9 speaks of those "from every nation, from all tribes and peoples and tongues, standing before the throne and before the Lamb, clothed in white robes...." The weight of these words is to stress the universality of those who are saved through the sacrifice of Jesus Christ.

The designation of the individual Chapels of the Tongues was influenced by the languages and nationalities most represented in New York at the turn of the century and by the major waves of immigrants in that era. Four architectural firms, each of them widely known and respected, were involved in the designs of these seven spaces set aside for the various immigrating nationalities. Each of the seven Chapels of the Tongues was a memorial given by a family, with the exception of St. Ansgar's, which was financed by public subscription and dedicated to the saintly Dr. William Reed Huntington. The chapters that follow give details on each apsidal chapel. The remainder of this chapter focuses on the artwork, plaques, and other adornments that highlight the ambulatory.

⒜ On a pillar to the left of the south entrance to the ambulatory is **the Levi Parsons Morton Plaque**, recognizing one of the largest gifts ever made to the Cathedral, a gift which paid for the entire structure above the choir, presbytery, and high altar. Morton's long life (1824–1920) included public service as governor of the State of New York and vice-president of the United States. He was the great great uncle of the Cathedral's seventh dean, James Parks Morton.

⒝ **The ambulatory gateways**, at the north and south entrances, are elaborately wrought steel creations thirty feet high. Made by Messrs. Warren and Wetmore under the direction of Cram and Ferguson, they were a gift of the Cathedral League and the Diocesan Auxiliary.

⒞ Entering the ambulatory from the south, one finds an alcove on the right in which is **the Muriel Rukeyser Poetry Wall**, named for the renowned poet who was an artist-in-residence at the time of her death in 1988. Original writings are placed there periodically. Some are the works of students at the Cathedral School. Others have been submitted by prisoners from throughout the nation. Visitors are welcome to take a prisoner's poem home if they will correspond with him or her. By so doing, the visitors are, in a modern way, fulfilling the mandate found in Matthew 25:39–40.

⒟ Opposite the poetry wall, at the higher level, are **the Madonna paintings**, including • *Madonna and Child with the Infant St. John the Baptist,* an early sixteenth-century Italian painting given by Miss Eleanor M. Mellon. The following were all given

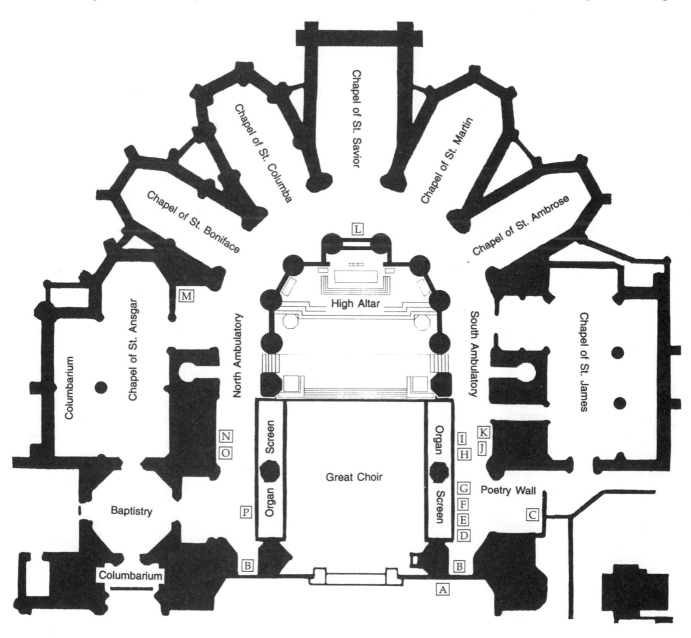

by the Reverend Robert J. Nevin, D.D.: • *Madonna and Child*, fifteenth-century Italian; • *Madonna and Child with St. John the Baptist and St. Peter*, early fifteenth-century Italian; • *Madonna and Child*, fifteenth-century Italian of the school of Antoniazzo Romano; and • *Madonna and Child with the Infant St. John the Baptist*, fifteenth-century Italian.

At a level beneath these paintings are:

E **The Healey Willan Plaque**, honoring the outstanding church musician from Canada.

F **The Lena Kearney Morton Plaque**, representing the gift of the Great Pipe Organ in her memory by her parents, Levi Parsons Morton and Anna Livingston Morton. (Details about the organ are presented on pp. 128–129.)

G **The Selwyn Plaque**, acknowledging the gifts and the signal role played by the first lord bishop of Auckland, New Zealand.

H Slightly to the right of these plaques is **the Belgian Porcelain**, a gift of King Albert in 1928. It is entitled *Descent from the Cross*.

I Further to the east on this same wall hang four panels of the sixteenth-century **Kulmbach Polyptych**, gifts in memory of the Right Reverend James Henry Darlington and Louise Bearns, his wife. They include: a sainted abbot receiving his miter; the Visitation; the Epiphany; and the last Mass and the burial of the abbot.

J Across from these works of art, against the south wall of the south ambulatory, is a copy of **the Constitution**, engraved in bronze and presented to the Cathedral by the Daughters of the American Revolution.

K Immediately to the left is a marble table given by Mr. and Mrs. George Arents. Above it is a seventeenth-century needlework picture, *The Adoration*, believed to have originated in Savoy, a gift in memory of Mrs. Edward King.

L Directly behind the high altar, protected by a medieval iron grille, is **the Founder's Tomb**, containing the earthly remains of Horatio Potter, sixth bishop of New York. This is consistent with long-standing tradition in which a cathedral's founder or patron is entombed in that place of highest honor. (St. Peter at the Roman basilica that bears his name; St. James at Santiago; St. Edward the Confessor at Westminster Abbey.)

The sarcophagus and the recumbent figure of the bishop at the top are of limestone as are the five figures in the niches of the facade (left to right: St. Edward the Confessor with crown, scepter, and orb; St. Remigius with cup and scourge; St. John the Divine with pen, book, and eagle; St. Isidore with miter, pallium, and crozier; and St. Theodosius wearing a coronet with a cross, holding a staff, and reading from a scroll).

M At the entrance to St. Ansgar's Chapel is **the chandelier**, thirty feet in height, made of hand-cut Bohemian glass. It was presented to the Cathedral by President Benes of the Republic of Czechoslovakia in 1927. See photo, p. 119.

N A few steps to the left, on the northern wall, is **the Choir Boys' Stone**. Carved by William Scott in a pier, it celebrates the contribution toward the construction of the Cathedral made by its young singers. The names of the eight charter members of the school (also members of the class of 1911) are shown.

O A few more steps to the west is a **Diptych of the Annunciation**, a fourteenth-century Sienese painting attributed to Simone Martini. Beneath it is a marble credenza, the gift of Mr. and Mrs. George Arents.

P The area abutting the lengthy organ screen on the south side of the north ambulatory is regularly used for exhibits of fine art, photography, or other artifacts.

Iron grill and entrance to Chapel of St. Columba   Cathedral Archives

Chapel of St. James – eastern end

The Chapel of St. James

The first chapel beyond the southern entrance to the apse is named for St. James the Apostle, the patron of Spain. It highlights the contributions of Spain to the Christian tradition. With a seating capacity of 25 and its own Aeolian-Skinner organ of 857 pipes, it is often used for weddings, funerals, and small worship services. Designed by Henry Vaughan, this chapel is the gift of Elizabeth Scriven Potter in loving memory of her husband, Henry Codman Potter, seventh bishop of New York, whose tomb and recumbent effigy are in the center bay of the right aisle.

The altar is of gray Knoxville, Tennessee marble. The central feature of the limestone **reredos** is [1] a relief representing the Transfiguration. It is sometimes covered by a religious banner. On the sides are statues of the four Evangelists with their individual emblems: [2] St. Matthew with the winged man; [3] St. Mark with the lion; [4] St. Luke with the ox; and [5] St. John with the eagle. Beneath is [6] a sculpture of the Nativity, flanked by emblems of the Passion: [7] the crown of thorns; [8] the pillar at which Christ was scourged; [9] the knotted scourge and sponge; [10] the hammer, coat, and three dice.

Chancel window (above reredos): The rosette [11] shows an angel surrounded by seven doves in the cusps. In the left lancet are [12] three angelic figures, one holding a floriated cross; [13] St. Michael and St. James; [14] three angels, one holding the cypher of the Virgin Mary. At the bottom of the central lancet are [15] two angels supporting a chalice. The remainder of that lancet is dominated by [16] Christ as described in the Revelation. In the right lancet are [17] an angel holding crossed palms; [18] an angel standing beside a kneeling St. John with the Bible open to the Fourth Gospel; [19] St. Catherine with the wheel (symbol of her martyrdom). Henry Wynd Young made this window.

The small southern window above the credence shows [20] St. James of Ulm, patron of glassmakers, with a glass-cutting scene below, and [21] St. Elroy, patron of ironworkers, with a blacksmith's shop below. This is also the work of Henry Wynd Young.

Window over sacristy door: The rosette consists of a trefoil showing [22] St. Christopher, [23] St. James, and [24] the Virgin of Guadalupe. The left lancet shows [25] Archbishop Toribio de Mogrovejo and Fra Diego Reynoso. In the center (as part of a scene that covers all three lancets) are [26] two Central American Indians. At the top [27] Fra Antonio Marchema and Fra Juan Pérez. In the center lancet are [28] Bartolomé de Las Casas, Apostle of the Indies, and Pedro de Alvarado; [29] Christopher Columbus kneeling after his arrival in America; [30] King Ferdinand and Queen Isabella giving Columbus support; [31] Cabeza de Vaca and an attendant; [32] Columbus's companions landing in the New World; [33] Columbus and his vision. This is another Henry Wynd Young creation.

Three large windows occupy the south wall. The rightmost features old Spain, its saints, scholars, and warriors: [34] Trajan and Hadrian, Roman emperors of Spanish birth; [35] St. Ildefonso, archbishop of Toledo; [36] Rodrigo di Vivar (El Cid); [37] Solomon Ibn Gabriol and Moses ben Ezra, poetic and philosophical writers; [38] Ferdinand, king of Castile; [39] St. Justa and St. Rufina, virgin martyrs; [40] Avempace and Averroes, Arab philosophers; [41] St. Leander and St. Isidore, bishops of Seville; [42] Hosius, bishop of Cordoba; [43] Marcus Aurelius and Theodosius, Roman emperors of Spanish origin; [44] St. Hermengild, martyr; [45] St. Eulalia and St. Leocadia, martyrs. The window is the work of Ernest Lakeman.

St. James, the patron of Spain, is the focus of **the center window** in still scenes and in moving narrative: [46] an angel with IC-XC (Greek abbreviation for Jesus Christ); [47] "Unto his shrine the mighty and the lowly fared on pilgrimage"; [48] "James, servant of God"; [49] "They bore his body to a ship that sailed for Spain"; [50] "St. James, radiant knight on a great white horse"; [51] "St. James preaches in Spain"; [52] "Over his

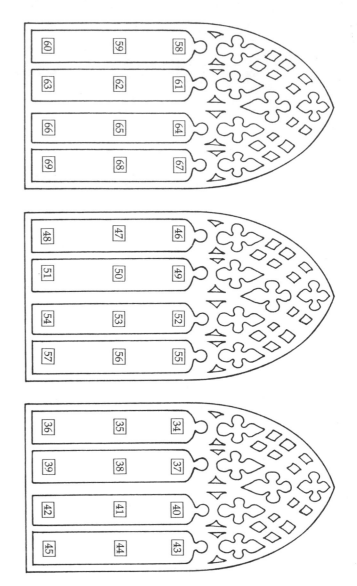

tomb they built a chapel"; 53 "Before the banner of his name the Moorish warriors fled"; 54 St. James before the judge, forgiving his accuser; 55 an angel with the *ichthus* (fish) symbol; 56 at "Compostela still men serve Santiago's shrine"; 57 the coat of arms of King Ramiro I. The window is by Henry Wynd Young.

The theme in **the left window** is Spain Reconquered, featuring Spanish artists, writers, and mystics: 58 Cervantes, Lope de Vega, and Calderón, dramatists; 59 St. John of the Cross, mystic; 60 Francisco de Osuna and Luis de Granada, theological writers; 61 St. Ignatius Loyola on his way to Rome, 62 as a soldier, and 63 holding his vigil at the altar of Our Lady of Montserrat; 64 vision of St. Teresa of Avila meeting the child, 65 St. Teresa holding the crown of thorns, and 66 St. Teresa teaching her nuns to pray; 67 El Greco and Murillo, painters; 68 St. Peter of Alcantara; and 69 Luis de León, Ramón Lull, and Juan de los Angeles, philosophical and theological writers. The window is by Ernest Lakeman.

Other Highlights

• There are carved statues and symbols as follows on the east wall: St. Augustine of Canterbury with a crozier (left) and St. Gregory the Great with a papal tiara and cross (right). • On the west wall, main aisle: Christ between St. Peter (left) and St. Paul (right). • At the west end of the south aisle, Venerable Bede; • a painting, *Ecce Homo*, by the sixteenth-century artist Luis de Morales; • a Flemish tapestry, the gift of Courtlandt Palmer; • three landscape paintings by Hayden Stubbing, a gift of the Lindisfarne Association; • two abstract landscapes by the late Australian painter Margery Edwards; and • a small carved donkey (sixteenth-century Spanish), which is carried in procession on Palm Sunday and Christmas, given in memory of dramatist Austin Strong.

 *Commentary*

The Patron and the Faith of Spain

St. James — son of Zebedee, brother of St. John, and disciple of Jesus — has been the patron saint of Spain since the early ninth century. In 813 it was reported in northwestern Spain that angels surrounded by stars had been sighted in a field. When the field was excavated, human bones were discovered in the soil. Since there was already a legend that St. James had spent several years in Roman Galacia after the Crucifixion and Resurrection, the local bishop declared these to be his bones. Never mind that the good saint had died a martyr in Israel; it was merely necessary to update the legend to include the miraculous transportation of the remains back to Spain.

However improbable or opportunistic this may seem to the modern mind, it captured the imagination of those living in the Iberian peninsula. For the next five centuries they fought under the saint's banner as they sought to repel the Moslems, shouting his name "Santiago," much as later warriors would cry "Geronimo." Credited with victories and absolved from defeats, St. James became known as "The Moorslayer."

The spot where the original angelic appearance had been reported was thereafter known as St. Iago de Campus Stellae (St. James of the Field of the Stars), which was eventually condensed into Santiago de Compostela. A church constructed over the relics was later replaced by a cathedral, which became the terminus of the most popular pilgrimage in Western Europe.

St. Francis made the holy trek, as did Sir Walter Raleigh and John of Gaunt. Louis VII of France and Ferdinand and Isabella of Spain were among the royalty who went with prayers of intercession and thanksgiving. Dante wrote, "Whoever is outside his fatherland is a pilgrim, whereas in a narrow sense one of us is not called a pilgrim unless he is journeying toward the sanctuary of St. James of Compostela or is returning therefrom."

A map of the pilgrim routes as they proceeded southwestward from France to Spain resembles the drainage system of a huge watershed. Once past the Pyrenees, the streams converge into a single east-west river known locally as the Camino Francés (French Road). Those on the homeward journey sported cockleshells (the symbol of St. James), emblematic proof of their achievement and a forerunner of today's decals and bumper stickers.

ଓଃ

The cult of St. James could have arisen only in a land that was already enthusiastically Christian. Whether or not it came with the Apostle in the first instance, it was one of the latter-day legacies of the Roman empire that succeeded in unifying the peninsula under the law and religion centered in Rome.

Iberia thrived for a while. However, along with the good roads and the good law, it acquired the same smug softness that made the entire empire vulnerable. In the wake of the Vandals came the Visigoths, who took over the nation and took on its religion. By the early seventh century two formidable non-Christian populations were growing in the land. The Jews, with the oldest faith on the Continent, came in peace — often as refugees. The Muslims, a new religious group, were just gaining muscularity. Having taken over the coastal portion of North Africa, they crossed the Straits of Gibraltar and gradually took over Spain by conversion as much as by conquest.

The history of the major house of worship in Cordoba tells much of the sequence of religious dominance in Spain. Visigothic Christians built a church that was, for a time, shared with conquering Muslims. But in the late 700s the church was replaced by an enormous mosque. More than six centuries later the city was recaptured by Christian forces; and in due course a cruciform church was built *within* the mosque. There it stands today, a sixteenth-century cathedral inside of an eighth-century mosque and still, ironically, called "La Mezquita" (The Mosque) by the locals.

In the early centuries of the second millennium Spain was the most religiously diverse nation in Europe; and there are some indications that this pluralism could and should have been preserved. In certain broad-minded sectors a policy of *convivencia* (roughly equivalent to détente or glasnost) existed between Muslims and Christians. Indeed, Spain's most popular warrior, Rodrigo di Vivar, was given his title, "El Cid," by admiring Muslims. El Cid's life, like that of Galahad in England and Roland in France, became the grain of sand around which a pearl of lore was formed.

Unfortunately, those with a rabid desire to Christianize the peninsula prevailed. The result was the Inquisition, an era of persecution and torture in which Jews were deported and Moors slowly driven out of the country. It is as sorry a chapter in Christian history as the Crusades that had taken place at the opposite end of the Mediterranean.

The period did, however, produce two Christians of towering stature and positive influence, St. Ignatius Loyola (1491–1556) founded the Society of Jesus (Jesuits), a religious order known for its brilliance, courage, and political intrigue. St. Teresa of Avila (1515–82) reformed and expanded the Carmelite nuns, an order that she felt had become too worldly. Both of these sixteenth-century saints have been declared doctors of the church by the Vatican. St. Teresa is one of only two women so honored to date (the other being St. Catherine of Siena). It is these two who are featured in the left window of the south wall of St. James Chapel.

Reredos – Chapel of St. James

G. Lynas

The Chapel of St. Ambrose

he second chapel on the south side of the ambulatory was planned with the Italian community in mind. In the early 1900s the Italians entering the United States outnumbered all other ethnic immigrants.

When the Cathedral's planners decided to set aside a chapel for Americans of Italian descent, they had a huge choice of saints upon which to draw. More than a third of all those canonized have been natives of Italy. The selection of Ambrose was not capricious, however. San Ambrogio was so popular in the land of his birth that the City of New York had already named the anchored light vessel marking the entrance to the harbor after this much beloved fourth-century bishop. St. John's was reinforcing this welcome.

Born in 340 C.E., Ambrose was the son of a Roman prefect. There is a cherished story that one day while he was in his cradle, a swarm of bees settled on his mouth but did him no harm. (A similar legend had been associated with Plato eight centuries earlier.) The incident was seen as an augury of greatness, and the beehive became Ambrose's most commonly used symbol.

Ambrose studied law at Rome and became governor of a province in northern Italy. His wisdom and skill were so overwhelming that on one occasion, when called upon to settle a dispute concerning the succession of the bishopric of Milan, he himself emerged as the compromise candidate, acceptable to both factions. A child is alleged to have started a popular chant, "Ambrose for bishop." The modest governor demurred, noting that he was only a catechumen in the church. However, he was hastily baptized and made bishop of Milan. In addition to a prodigious output of writings, which resulted in his designation as one of the four Latin doctors of the church, he had a profound influence on a young African whose fame would eventually surpass his own: Augustine.

ଔ

The chapel, designed in modern Renaissance style, is the work of Carrere and Hastings, the architects of the New York Public Library. The floor is inlaid with grey Siena, red Verona, and cream-colored Cenere marbles. On the underside of the marble archway of the entrance are reliefs representing the Three Persons of the Trinity amid angels.

The side walls are lined with Rosato marble and highlighted by trompe l'oeil arches, which appear much deeper than their actual six inches of depth. This artistic deception was inspired by a similar effect on the walls of the sacristy at the Cathedral of Siena.

In **the spandrels** (curved triangles) above the false arches in the left wall are represented (reading from entrance toward altar) Moses, Isaiah, Jeremiah, and Ezekiel. In the spandrels of the right wall arches, reading in the same direction, are St. Matthew with the angel, St. Mark with the lion, St. Luke with the ox, and St. John with the eagle. From the ceiling hang four silver lamps, one of them an antique Italian lamp, the others reproductions of it.

The reredos above the altar, based on transitional and early Renaissance styles in Italy, is carved of wood and gesso (artists' plaster of paris) overlaid with gold leaf. The lower part consists of a triptych covered with an elaborate canopy and flanked by niches in which are statues of St. Francis of Assisi (left) and St. Ambrose (right). Above, in the niches at the left of the canopy are (left to right) St. Benedict, St. Agnes, and Dante. Continuing on the right side are Fra Angelico, Galileo, and Savonarola. Above the cross of the canopy is a dove, symbolizing God the Holy Ghost; above that is the all-seeing eye in a triangle within a sunburst, symbolizing God the Father; and topmost is the figure of God the Son, holding a cross and giving a blessing.

Since the two windows contain almost no pictorial representations, a diagram is unnecessary. The

St. Ambrose Chapel

A. Leonard Gustafson

panes of **the left window** are ornamented with repeated designs showing the chalice with the emerging serpent and eagle (symbols of St. John), flowers, and the Chi-Rho monogram (the first two letters of the word "Christ" in Greek). Near the top, and centered, is the Cathedral's insignia.

The designs in **the right window** are repetitions of the beehive, miter, and scourges (symbols of St. Ambrose) plus a cross, a wreath, and flowers. There are two Greek inscriptions: IC-XC (the first and last letters of "Jesus" and "Christ") and IHS (the first three letters of "Jesus"). In the center, near the top, is St. Ambrose's insignia. The windows were made by Henry Wynd Young under the supervision of Godwin and Sullivan, New York architects.

Along **the side walls** are stalls and wainscoting of dark Italian walnut, inlaid with pearwood. The top border of the wainscoting carries scriptural quotes from the Old and New Testament.

Plaques on either side of the chapel entrance mention that the main donor was Sara Whiting Rives in memory of members of the Whiting and Rives families, plus other gifts given later in memory of Mrs. Rives.

Other Highlights

Several fine Italian paintings from the most prolific period of religious art (1450–1650) adorn the chapel walls. • There are two works of art by Domenichino, the gifts of Katherine W. Burch. • *The Annunciation* by Sabbatini appears as a gift from Electa and Laura McKey in memory of their brother, Edward Michael McKey. • *The Baptism of Christ*, which hangs in the chapel's eastern entrance, is from the atelier of the brother and sons of Paolo Caliari (Paul Veronese). It is a gift of F. Kleinberger. • *The Virgin and Child*, attributed to Perugino, is the gift of the nephews of Robert J. Nevin, D.D. • In a niche at the rear of the chapel is a nineteenth-century Roman bronze statue of St. John the Baptist, the gift of Mrs. Irving McKesson. • The two Renaissance angelic figures holding candlesticks were donated by Mrs. Murray Young; and the two kneeling angels, also sixteenth century, came from Mrs. Simon Guggenheim. • The Belgian government contributed the sanctuary lamp before the altar in 1928. • The statue of St. Anthony, which rests upon the credence, was sculpted by Luca Della Robbia and donated by Mrs. Louis Sather Brugiere. Beneath is a carved Renaissance

Baptism of Christ

marriage cassone, the gift of Mrs. Simon Guggenheim. • The antique candlesticks on the credence came from Mrs. Ludlow Bull. • The free-standing Renaissance choir stalls came originally from Spoleto, Italy, and were later donated by the Rossin family. • The ornate bronze screen at the chapel entrance should be viewed from within the chapel. It was designed by Carrere and Hastings and executed by the E. F. Caldwell Company of New York. It contains seven scenes in the life of St. Ambrose, left to right: a child shouting "Ambrose for bishop"; the settling of the succession of the bishopric of Milan; his baptism; monks and nuns listening to his preaching; the public penance of Emperor Theodosius the Great before St. Ambrose; the laying of the cornerstone of the Church of San Ambrogio in Milan; and his death. Beneath the figure of St. Ambrose at the very center of the screen is his most common symbol, the beehive, with crossed pastoral staves.

 *Commentary*

The Role of Rome

In one sense it seems ironic that Rome should have become the dominant city of Christendom. It was Romans who crucified Jesus Christ and persecuted his followers for nearly three centuries. And Rome was manifestly the external enemy alluded to in St. John's Revelation.

But despite the blindness and brutality of many of its officials, Rome and its empire played a positive part in the spread of the new faith. The Apostle Peter, recognizing the importance of the imperial city, made his way there and is regarded as the first of nearly three hundred popes. His colleague, Mark, penned the first Gospel from that city on the Tiber. And Paul, the irrepressible convert, wrote his most powerful letter to the growing Christian community there.

Furthermore, as noted elsewhere in these pages, it was due to Roman roads, soldiers, and traders that the Gospel had spread throughout Western Europe long before Constantine the Great officially ended the persecutions. Was that emperor motivated by his mother, St. Helena, or by his vision of the Cross in the Battle of Milvian Bridge (312), or by the political instinct to go with a winner? Perhaps a combination. In any event, all subsequent Roman emperors, with exception of Julian, were Christians, and the empire changed from persecutor to promoter of the faith.

Another contribution of the highly developed culture emanating from the great peninsula in the Mediterranean was the introduction of "left brain" thinking to a religion that had been driven largely by faith and emotion. Law, which the Romans had advanced to a new level, was helpful in adjudicating between factions and charges of heresy that arose among second- and third-century Christians. Subsequently, leaders such as Jerome, Augustine of Hippo, Ambrose, and Gregory helped to give Christianity a theological structure beyond the ken or imaginings of the humble martyrs whose faith had ignited the movement.

As the hub of organized Christianity, Rome survived the decline of the empire primarily because many of the tribes that replaced that empire converted to the faith. The city's preeminence as the ultimate source of authority was somewhat diminished by the split with Eastern Orthodoxy in the eleventh century and the Protestant and Anglican Reformations in the sixteenth and seventeenth centuries. Still Christendom has no other city that rivals it in influence and no leader or ecclesiastical position with the visibility or clout of Rome's bishop, the pope.

The papacy has been headquartered in Rome from its beginning, except for a brief span (1309–77) in Avignon, France. Perhaps as a consequence, a majority of the popes have been Italian. The Vatican, an enclave within the city, includes the pope's residence, St. Peter's Basilica, the Sistine Chapel, and the worldwide headquarters of the Roman Catholic Church. This 110-acre precinct gained absolute independence and sovereignty as a state in an agreement signed by Benito Mussolini in 1929.

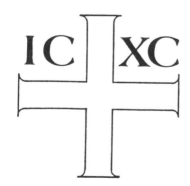

Abbreviations for the names "Jesus" and "Christ"
in Greek letters. See text at top of p. 107.

The Chapel of St. Martin

The Chapel of St. Martin of Tours, the third of those in the south ambulatory, was designed with French immigrants in mind. It is the Cathedral's Chapel of Reservation. This means that it is set aside for private devotions and is not included on any tour for visitors. Here the consecrated bread and wine and the oils for healing are kept (see the description of the aumbrey below). Designed by Cram and Ferguson, its style is thirteenth-century Gothic. The pavement is Tennessee pink marble bordered by Belgian black marble.

The interior walls are faced with Indiana limestone. The lower half of these walls consists of decorative Gothic arcature surmounted by medieval texts and fleurs-de-lis. The upper portion consists of an unusual triforium gallery built to the thickness of the walls.

The following essay, "Gallic Christianity," may be helpful in appreciating the depictions in stained glass, statuary, and the iron screen.

Windows

The seven windows of this chapel were made by Charles J. Connick of Boston. The three apsidal windows, the ones with pictorial scenes, show the following:

Center: [1] St. Martin receives a sword and enters the army, [2] divides his cloak with a beggar, [3] sees Christ wearing half of the cloak, and [4] is baptized. [5] St. Martin converts a robber, [6] revives a dead man, [7] is welcomed in Tours, and [8] destroys a heathen temple. Finally, [9] he intercedes for the release of a prisoner, [10] pleads for Priscillian's life, [11] dies, and [12] his body is borne away by ship. (It is actually buried in Tours.)

Left (only the center lancet contains scenes): [13] St. Louis is crowned, [14] releases prisoners, [15] ministers to sick soldiers on the Seventh Crusade, and [16] dies during the Eighth Crusade.

Right (center lancet only): [17] Saint Joan of Arc's vision, [18] the capture of Orleans, [19] the coronation of Charles VII, and [20] St. Joan's martyrdom in Rouen.

Other Features

• At the left end of the chapel apse is a statue of Joan of Arc by Anna Hyatt Huntington. It was given by J. Sanford Saltus through Dr. George Kunz, president of the Joan of Arc Statue Committee, which erected on Riverside Drive the equestrian statue of the Maid by the same sculptor. Beneath is a rough stone from the Rouen cell in which the Maid was imprisoned and from which she was led to the stake.

• The marble altar, in the form of a table resting on red marble pillars, is free-standing.

• In the center of the stone trefoil above the altar cross is embedded a fragment of stone that fell from Rheims Cathedral during its bombardment in World War I. It was a gift to the Cathedral from Cardinal Mercier.

• At the left rear corner of the chapel is a great Sèvres vase, presented by the French government in 1925.

• The aumbrey (a locked cupboard or safe for keeping the Blessed Sacrament) is to the left of the altar. The front is carved oak, gilded and polychromed. The ornamentation consists of a chalice and host at the top and a Calvary on the door, below which is St. Martin on horseback, dividing his cloak with the beggar.

• The wrought-iron screen separating the chapel from the ambulatory contains a shell ornament below the cornice, symbolic of St. Martin as a pilgrim. In the frieze are four panels depicting familiar scenes from his life and described in the molding above.

• Against the wall is an eighteenth-century French statue of the Blessed Virgin Mary and Child in polychromed wood. This was the gift of Carol Penney Guyer in memory of her husband, David Guyer.

 *Commentary*

Gallic Christianity

Like the other major sectors of Western Europe, Gaul first received the Gospel by way of the trade and military routes radiating from Rome.

By the mid-third century, the Franks had their first martyr, St. Denis. Denis had been commissioned by the pope to convert the heathen to the northwest. He did indeed win converts; but others were intimidated by him and he was beheaded in 250. His body, recovered from the Seine River, provided relics for a series of churches bearing his name. St. Denis became the nation's first patron.

In the following century another Roman, Martin by name, went to Gaul. According to legend, he encountered a naked beggar by the roadside one wintry day, took a sword, and rent his own cloak in twain, giving half to the beggar. Later, in a vision, he saw Christ wearing the half cloak and proclaiming, "Know ye who hath thus arrayed me? My servant, Martin, though yet unbaptized, has done this." Baptism came shortly thereafter and then holy orders. Ultimately Martin became bishop of Tours where tales of his special powers and kindliness abounded. After his death in 397, his tomb became a favorite point of pilgrimage.

From a governmental standpoint, the conversion of Clovis, the Frankish king, and his baptism at Rheims on Christmas 497 was a milestone. Widely considered the nation's first king, Clovis eventually bequeathed the name of his Frankish people to the entire country. Rheims served as the coronation city for the next millennium, and Clovis's name in derivative form (Louis) was later chosen by a host of French monarchs.

One of those namesakes, Louis IX, had the unique distinction of being a monarch, a Crusader, and a saint. He led two unsuccessful Crusades, dying in the second, but became the most beloved and admired figure of his era. His friend, Thomas Aquinas, overshadowed him in intellect and lasting contributions to the faith; but Louis gave humankind a beatific example. The rarest of rarities, a humble king, he promoted almsgiving, founded a hospital for the poor, witnessed against capital punishment, and insisted that justice be administered without respect to wealth or social class. Nor was his demeanor altered by the pressures of battle, defeat, and capture. He continued to minister physically and spiritually to his soldiers. A scant twenty-seven years after his death in 1270, Louis was canonized.

Only one French saint was to surpass Louis in popularity. In many ways she was an improbable candidate: an illiterate peasant girl who heard voices inaudible to all others and was put to death by the church while still a teenager. Joan of Arc was born in Domrémy in 1412. Through the power of personality and some prophecies that were quickly fulfilled, she persuaded a reluctant Dauphin to support her in an attack on the occupying English forces in Orleans.

History offers few pictures more stirring than the image of this spirited, androgynous youngster, clad in white armor, riding at the head of the cavalry, and inspiring fellow French to recapture their city. The Dauphin's faith in her paid handsomely; and when, shortly thereafter, he was crowned as Charles VII in Rheims Cathedral, Joan had her moment of triumph. Then followed battle losses, capture, trial, and condemnation as a witch and false prophet. No help came from the king; and on May 30, 1431, she was burned at the stake in Rouen.

It took centuries for the church to yield to public sentiment and overrule the stand of the French bishop on the Maid of Orleans. She was canonized in 1920, just in time for George Bernard Shaw to write *Saint Joan*.

The English were finally driven from the mainland and the Hundred Years War (which in fact lasted

St. Joan of Arc statue – Chapel of St. Martin   G. Lynas

115 years) ended in 1453. Within a few decades, however, a different kind of struggle erupted that, with periodic truces, lasted two and a half centuries. This was a religious war, a war for human souls and for the earthly power that so often accrues to religious institutions.

The Reformation came as an affront and threat to the established church of France. That institution had become the nation's major landlord and richest institution. Suddenly a group of purists, called "Huguenots" and inspired by the writings of Martin Luther in Germany, began to proselytize and preach reform.

Reform is never popular with those in ascendancy; and the Church of Rome fully supported the leadership of France in meeting this challenge with force. The first Huguenot martyrdom came in 1523, but it was another decade before the movement catalyzed around John Calvin, a lawyer/theologian from Picardy. The flight of Calvin and his supporters to Geneva, Switzerland, gave birth to the word "refugee"; and the subsequent teachings of this group added "Calvinism" to the vocabulary and spectrum of Christianity.

For more than two hundred years there were skirmishes, repressions, and killings, of which the St. Bartholomew Massacre (1572) was the most infamous. Pacts such as the Edict of Nantes (1598) and the Peace of Utrecht (1713) brought periods of détente and quiescence; but it was not until Voltaire took up the cause of an executed Protestant (1762) that the martyrdoms were over.

Although the Roman Church had prevailed, French Christianity suffered as the result of the protracted war with the Huguenots. Gone was that vitality that comes from challenge and diversity. The vigor of Gaul in later times has been channeled more toward politics whereas the dynamism of the church has waned.

A small percentage of the populace remains devout. Perhaps like the remnant of Israel they can preserve the beliefs and traditions until their compatriots return to them. When the racing fans at Le Mans grow jaded and yearn for something more valuable than fast cars, the great cathedral of that city will be waiting for them. And when the artificial lights of Paris pall, Parisians may again seek the light of God at Notre Dame, Sacré-Coeur, St. Denis, St. Eustache, and dozens of other houses of worship bequeathed to them from the Middle Ages.

St. Savior Chapel

The Chapel of St. Savior

irectly behind the high altar is a chapel dedicated to Christian communities of the East. Gradually it came to focus on the art and symbols of the Orthodox churches (see the essays following) and has often been used by Orthodox fellowships that lacked worship facilities. Appropriately located at the easternmost part of the Cathedral, it is named St. Savior Chapel. The designation may sound awkward or redundant to those who think of "saint" only as a title (like "president" or "doctor"). In this instance, however, "saint" is used in its primary sense as an adjective, derived from the Latin *sanctus*, meaning "holy." This, then, is Holy Savior Chapel, just as the East's most famous church building, St. Sophia, is dedicated to Holy Wisdom.

Completed in 1904 by Heins and LaFarge, this chapel stood alone for several years as the first portion of the huge cathedral. During that period it was referred to as "the Belmont Chapel" since it had been given by August Belmont in memory of his wife. Because the Orthodox emphasis had not been specifically chosen at the outset, an English Decorated Gothic style was chosen. However, the icons and the figures of Eastern doctors and saints in sculpture and stained glass clearly set the desired tone.

The walls are of Minnesota dolomite; around their base runs a foundation stratum of red jasper with green molding. The pavement is of stone from Hauteville, France, with a mosaic border. The steps to the altar are of pink marble from Georgia, and the altar is of white Carrara marble.

Above is a **large window** (by Hardman of Birmingham, England), which fills the eastern end of the chapel. The left lancet features Moses ① removing his shoes by the burning bush and ② raising the brazen serpent for healing. The large central light shows ③ the Transfiguration. The transfigured Lord is flanked by Moses holding the Ten Commandments and Elijah holding the receptacle of the scrolls. Together they represent the Law and the Prophets. Beneath, left to right, are Saints Peter, James, and John. Elijah is the subject of the right lancet as he ④ be-

holds the angel and ⑤ has his sacrifice miraculously consumed by the fire of the Lord.

In **the niches** on either side of the window are statues of bishops, saints, and scholars of the Eastern church as follows: On the left side ⑥ St. Polycarp, bishop of Smyrna and martyr; ⑦ St. Athanasius, bishop of Alexandria and doctor of the church; ⑧ Origen, great scholar; and ⑨ St. Gregory Nazianzen, bishop of Nazianzus and doctor of the church. On the right side ⑩ St. John Chrysostom, bishop of Constantinople and doctor of the church; ⑪ St. Basil, bishop of Caesarea and doctor of the church; ⑫ St. Clement of Alexandria, writer of the early church; and ⑬ St. Ignatius, bishop of Antioch and Apostolic Father.

Note that the four doctors included above were the Eastern counterparts of the four Latin Doctors (Gregory the Great, Ambrose, Augustine, and Jerome). For almost a thousand years those eight men were the only saints to be given that honorific title.

Other Highlights

• The entrance to the chapel is flanked by twenty carvings of angels, representing the heavenly choir. These were created by Gutzon Borglum (best known for the presidential faces he carved at Mt. Rushmore through the use of explosives). A minor controversy arose when he depicted the angels as females, contrary to the male tradition extending back to Michael, Gabriel, Uriel, Raphael, etc.

• The wrought-iron screen at the entrance is the work of W. H. Jackson Company of New York. Modeled after a similar screen in Orvieto, Italy, it is embellished by two golden angels holding a wreath at the foot of the Cross.

• Prominent within the chapel are four lamp stands of Carrara marble surmounted by alabaster bowls. They were created by F. Ruggeri and P. Giuntini. The sanctuary lamp hanging before the altar contains a traditional ostrich egg, the gift of P. L. Travers, who wrote *Mary Poppins*.

• The south (right) wall is a shrine of special significance. It was blessed by the Coptic pope, Abuna Theophilus, patriarch of Ethiopia, at the installation of the Cathedral's seventh dean, the Very Rev. James Parks Morton, on May 20, 1973. Soon afterward, that pope, along with other church leaders, was martyred in the military coup that deposed the Emperor Haile Selassie. The shrine is dedicated to four saints of Africa: St. Philip, St. George, St. Teklehaimanot, and St. Frumentius. Coming at the outset of a new era, this recognition of Africa's contribution to the Christian heritage signaled an expanded embrace in a Cathedral that had always sought to be global in outreach but had, in fact, focused largely on European church history. The central icon of the shrine, "The Lion of Judah and the Journey of the Queen of Sheba," is by the Ethiopian painter Girma Belachew.

Also part of the shrine is a group of twelve small icons representing (left to right): St. John Chrysostom (a seventeenth-century Russian work of art given by Father Peter Popoff), St. John the Divine, the burial of Christ, St. Luke, St. Spiridon, St. Demetrius, St. Charalampos, St. Tryphon, the Anastasis (Resurrection), Constantine and St. Helena (his mother), St. Salome, and St. Nicholas. The latter five, eighteenth-century Greek icons, were gifts of the heirs of the Right Reverend James Henry Darlington.

• Directly across, on the left (north) wall is a memorial to Athenagoras, late ecumenical patriarch of the Orthodox Church. Placed there by the National Council of Churches in 1973, it is a recognition of that prelate's great friendship with the Cathedral family.

• A number of other outstanding icons have been donated to the Cathedral. These are not hung in fixed positions; but they can usually be seen within this chapel or on the choir screen that serves as an iconostasis in the narthex.

• In a niche in the upper part of the north wall is a statue of St. Peter with a key; and in a corresponding niche in the south wall is St. Paul represented with a sword. Both were sculpted by Gutzon Borglum.

• On either side of the sanctuary (altar area) are Buddhist temple cabinets of gilded teakwood, given to the Cathedral in 1930 by the king of Siam.

Gate of the Chapel of St. Savior

 *Commentary*  *Commentary*

Choirs of Angels

Angels were taken very seriously in the Middle Ages, too seriously at times. Although they were believed to be immaterial (without physical bodies), a theological debate once arose as to how many of them could stand on the head of a pin.

The word "angel" derives from the Greek word for "messenger." It has come to describe a celestial entity that predated the earth's creation. According to the legend, God gave free will to the angels before the beginning of time. Some chose evil and became fallen angels. Condemned to eternal damnation, they are headed by the Prince of Darkness, whose aliases include Satan, the Devil, Lucifer, and Beelzebub.

Based on Isaiah 6:1–2 and Ezekiel 1:4–14, the concept of angels gained complexity as it grew. Subdivisions developed, nine of them. These ranks were called "choirs." Thus there is a pun in the words from the Christmas hymn, "Sing choirs of angels . . ." since "choirs" refers to categories as well as choral groups.

The top cluster of choirs — seraphim, cherubim, and thrones — were called counsellors. Next came the three choirs of governors of the stars and elements: dominions, virtues, and powers. Furthest from the top but closest to humankind were the messengers: principalities, archangels, and angels. ("Angel" is both the generic term for all of these heavenly beings and the specific title of the lowest of the nine choirs).

Another medieval belief rooted in Judaism held that each devout person had a guardian angel. Tobias, the righteous Jew, had been protected by the Archangel Raphael. Probably the most easily identifiable client of any guardian angel was Archangel Michael's Michelangelo.

In the fullness of time we will probably discover that heaven is quite different from the imaginings of mere mortals. Perhaps the gates are not encrusted with pearls nor the streets paved with gold. Meantime, we can do no better than to project our loftiest fantasies against the great unknown awaiting us. And angels remain key figures in that idealized scenario.

The Christian Tradition in the East

Technically, there was no schism within Christendom during its first millennium. The breech between East and West became formal and official in 1054. However, distinctions and disputes between the churches at the east end of the Mediterranean and those radiating from Rome had been mounting for centuries. Some seemed minor (the proper dates for celebrating Christmas and Easter); others were doctrinal (did the Holy Spirit descend from the Father or from the Father *and the Son?*); and some involved proper ecclesiastical practices (in the East, only bishops and monks are celibate; all parish priests are married).

When Pope Leo IX realized that the Eastern churches were becoming, in his point of view, increasingly independent and that the direction seemed irreversible, he made a preemptive strike by excommunicating the patriarch of Constantinople, much in the manner of a boss who shouts at a departing employee, "You can't quit; I'm firing you."

The affected churches labeled themselves "Orthodox," indicating their belief that they were doing things the *right* way. It was the Christians to the west who added the adjective "Eastern" to the title. And because the Orthodox Greeks outnumber those of other nationalities in the United States, "Greek Orthodox" is often incorrectly used as a generic term covering all of the cooperating but independent Eastern churches (Russian, Ukrainian, Syrian, Serbian, Bulgarian, Romanian, Albanian, Coptic, Armenian, and Greek).

Figures released prior to the return of religious freedom in Russia showed 165 million members worldwide in the various Orthodox churches as compared to approximately 70 million Anglicans, 370 million Protestants, and 1 billion Roman Catholics. Generally speaking, the Eastern churches are more mystical and less aggressive than the Anglican, Protestant, or Catholic divisions of Christendom.

Chapel of St. Columba

A. Leonard Gustafson

The Chapel of St. Columba

The church leaders who at the end of the nineteenth century selected St. Columba's name for the Cathedral's British chapel were politically astute. Each of Britain's components has its own patron: England: St. George; Scotland: St. Andrew; Wales: St. David; and Ireland: St. Patrick. To pick one of them would have been injudicious.

Furthermore, Columba is a much more full-blown historical figure than any of the other four. Patrick and David are the beneficiaries of legend and lore. Little is known about them except that neither was born in the nation that claims him. Saints Andrew and George never reached Western Europe, much less the British Isles, though relics of St. Andrew are said to repose in Fife, Scotland.

St. Columba (521–97) was born in Ireland and founded monasteries in Derry, Durrow, and Kells before traveling to the island of Iona off the western coast of Scotland. The monastery that he established there was for a time the foremost foundation of its kind in Britain and remains a renowned point of pilgrimage and visitation. Scholar, diplomat, and preacher, Columba used Iona as a base for missionary work throughout Scotland, Ireland, and northern England. He is considered foremost of the Celtic saints who were spreading the faith long before Augustine arrived from Rome to "Christianize" England. (See pp. 155–156 for further discussion of Celtic Christianity.)

CB

The Chapel of St. Columba, built by Heins and La-Farge and completed in 1911, was the second unit of the Cathedral to be constructed. The style is Norman/Romanesque with decorated cylindrical pillars that evoke Durham Cathedral, the finest Norman structure extant. The interior walls are of Minnesota dolomite, separated from a base course of Mohegan granite by a molding of yellow Verona marble. The pavement is a fine-grained gray stone from Illinois. The chapel was the gift of Mary Augusta King in loving memory of her daughter, Mary LeRoy King.

On the altar rests an outstanding fifteenth-century **polyptych** by Giovanni di Paolo (1403–82), the gift of Robert J. Nevin D.D. The figures, reading from the left, are St. John the Baptist (with St. Anne above); St. Peter (St. Agatha above); Madonna and Child (Christ above); St. Paul (St. Francis above); and St. Philip (St. Bernadine of Siena above).

The three windows of the chapel are purely decorative grisaille. The central window, which rises above the altar, was the work of Wilbur Herbert Burnham of Boston. The windows flanking it were made by Clayton and Bell of London and were inspired by the famous Five Sisters windows in the north transept of Yorkminster.

The wrought-iron screen at the entrance was designed by Samuel Yellin and executed by his Industrial Ornamental Iron Works Company of Philadelphia.

There are **ten statues** on each side of the entrance, all designed by Gutzon Borglum. They represent key figures in the development of Christianity in Britain and are placed according to chronology, reading from top to bottom. The ten that can be viewed from within the chapel are, *left:* St. Aidan, bishop and missionary, seventh century; St. Anselm, archbishop and theologian, eleventh century; Thomas Cranmer, archbishop and martyr (1489–1556); Joseph Butler, bishop and philosopher (1692–1752); John Keble, priest and scholar (1792–1866). *Right:* St. Augustine, first archbishop of Canterbury (d. 604); King Alfred, monarch and churchman (849–900); William of Wykeham, bishop and builder (1367–1405); Jeremy Taylor, bishop and pastor (1613–67); Reginald Heber, bishop and missionary (1783–1826).

Seen from the ambulatory, *Left:* St. Alban, protomartyr of Britain (d. 304); the Venerable Bede, priest and historian (d. 735); John Wycliffe, priest and reformer (1325–84); Richard Hooker, priest and theologian (1554–1600); John Wesley, priest and reformer (1703–91). *Right:* St. Theodore of Tarsus, archbishop (602–90); Stephen Langton, archbishop (1150–1228); Matthew Parker, archbishop (1504–75); George Berkeley, bishop and philosopher (1684–1753); Frederick Denison Maurice, theologian (1805–72).

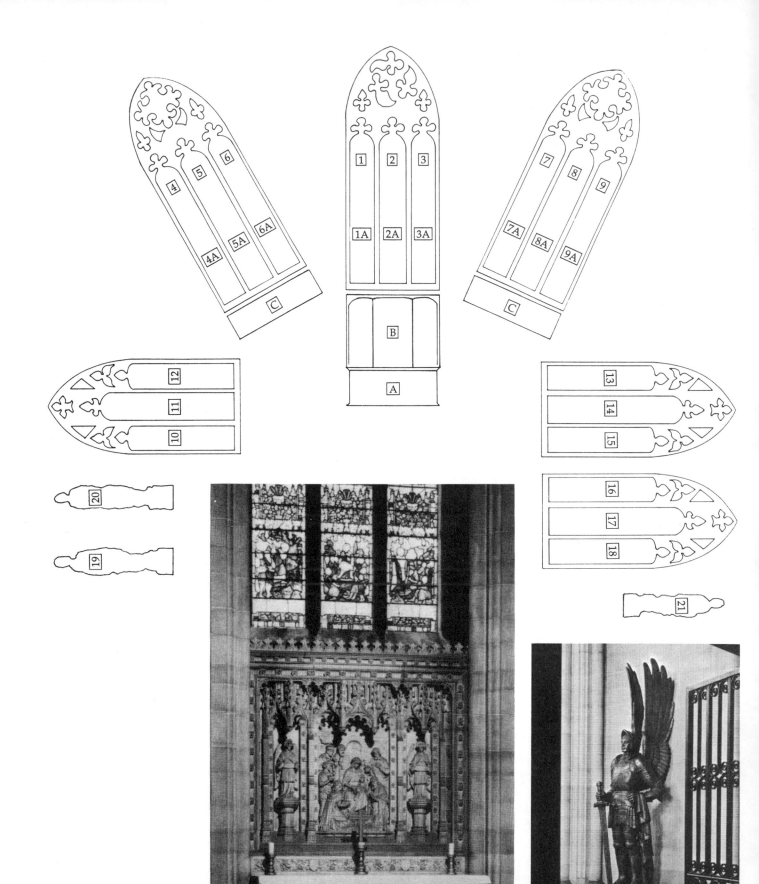

Altar, raredos, and window of Chapel of St. Boniface

St. Michael in bronze

The Chapel of St. Boniface

In the year 680 C.E. a baby was born in Devonshire, England, and baptized "Winfrid." By the end of the century he had entered a monastery. Shortly after being ordained a priest, he was sent by Pope Gregory to evangelize the tribes of Germany. When he found the natives worshiping nature, he promptly chopped down their most sacred tree. No ill befell him at the time and the conversions began. The pope rewarded him with a new name, "Boniface" (doer of good, *boni facio*). In 755 he was slain by unconverted heathen and eventually he gained his present title: Apostle (patron saint) of Germany.

The second chapel beyond the baptistry in the northern part of the ambulatory is named for St. Boniface and dedicated to Americans of German descent. Unfortunately, the windows and statues give little attention to Germany's contribution to the Christian faith, bypassing such giants as Martin Luther and Johann Sebastian Bach, focusing instead on British saints. This deficiency is seldom apparent, however, since the chapel is often used for contemporary art exhibits that command prime attention.

The gift of the George Sullivan Bowdoin family, this is one of three apsidal chapels designed by Henry Vaughan. The pavement, sanctuary steps, and Ⓐ altar are made of Knoxville marble. Above the altar is Ⓑ a carved reredos, showing the Adoration of the Magi, flanked by two angels with scrolls. On either side of the altar are Ⓒ clergy stalls carved of dark oak.

Each of the three windows surrounding the altar has three lancets, each with a major figure at the top and a scene below. In **the center window** are ① St. Boniface and ①Ⓐ the scene in which he hews down the tree sacred to the local idolators; ② Christ with angels and doves and ②Ⓐ Christ teaching the multitudes; and ③ St. Paul, shown ③Ⓐ preaching in Athens.

In **the left window** are ④ St. Birinus, bishop of Dorchester, ④Ⓐ shown baptizing the king of the West Saxons; ⑤ St. Augustine of Canterbury with his archiepiscopal staff, ⑤Ⓐ shown preaching to King Ethelbert; and ⑥ St. Felix, bishop of Dunwich, ⑥Ⓐ shown receiving the blessing of the archbishop of Canterbury.

In **the right window** are ⑦ St. Chad, bishop of Lichfield, ⑦Ⓐ holding a model of Lichfield Cathedral; ⑧ St. Columba in monastic garb, ⑧Ⓐ shown converting the Picts; and ⑨ St. Aidan with a pastoral staff, ⑨Ⓐ instructing a youthful St. Chad and others.

In **the small western window** are ⑩ St. Patrick with his pastoral staff ornamented with shamrocks, ⑪ St. Gregory of Rome with a papal staff and open book displaying the Sursum Corda, ⑫ and St. Martin of Tours with a pastoral staff and Bible.

Crystal chandelier in ambulatory   Cathedral Archives

[119]

In **the eastern wall** are two small windows. In the left are ☐13 St. Cyprian, bishop of Carthage; ☐14 St. Ambrose of Milan with a book displaying the words "Te Deum Laudamus" (We praise thee, O God), with missionary Robert Hunt below; and ☐15 St. Augustine, bishop of Hippo, with a pastoral staff.

In the right window of the east wall are ☐16 St. Cyril of Alexandria with book and staff; ☐17 St. John Chrysostom with staff, chalice, and book of homilies, with Congregationalist missionary John Robinson below; and ☐18 St. Ignatius, bishop of Antioch, holding a palm.

In the two canopied **niches of the west wall** are statues of ☐19 Thomas à Kempis and ☐20 St. Boniface. The single niche of the east wall shows ☐21 the scholar Erasmus.

All of the windows of this chapel were made by C. E. Kempe and Company of London, which may explain the heavy emphasis on Britishers.

Other Features

• At the entrance is a wrought-iron screen adorned with escutcheons bearing the IHC monogram of Jesus and surmounted by a floriated cross.

• The bronze statue of St. Michael the Archangel, nearly a ton in weight, is the work of Eleanor Mellon. The figure itself is eight feet tall and the full distance from base to wingtops is eleven feet.

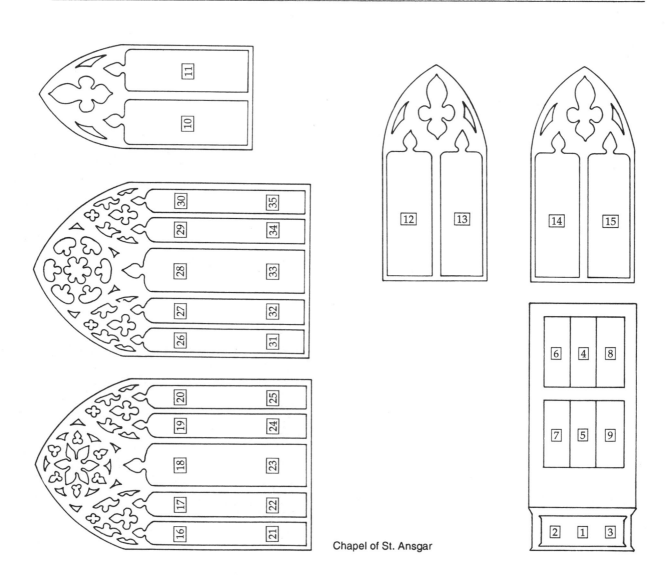

Chapel of St. Ansgar

The Chapel of St. Ansgar

Born in Amiens, France, in 801, Ansgar became the first archbishop of Hamburg and Bremen. From that base he made many missionary tours into Denmark and Sweden and eventually became known as "The Apostle of the North." St. Ansgar's Chapel, immediately east of the baptistry, was planned to meet the spiritual needs of Scandinavian Christians. It has been frequently used for art exhibitions.

Like St. James Chapel at the opposite side of the apse, St. Ansgar's is double sized, has its own pipe organ, and was designed by Henry Vaughan. The interior walls are of Indiana limestone.

On the front of **the altar,** which is carved of Tennessee marble, are ① the Madonna of the Chair, flanked by ② St. Michael with the sword and ③ St. Gabriel with lilies of the Annunciation. In the center of the sculptured **reredos** ④ Christ is shown holding the orb of sovereignty; beneath is ⑤ Christ's baptism by St. John Baptist. To the left are ⑥ St. Ansgar with a pastoral staff and ⑦ Gustavus Adolphus. At the right are ⑧ St. Olaf and ⑨ Martin Luther. In the small windows above the altar are shown ⑩ St. Willibrord with a miter; ⑪ St. Canute with crown, scepter, and sword; ⑫ St. Ansgar with a miter; ⑬ St. Olaf with crown and scepter; ⑭ St. Eric; and ⑮ St. Wilfrid.

In the two bays of the north aisle are two large stained-glass windows, each having five lights and each light depicting two scenes.

The left, or western, window shows Old Testament figures in the top row:

⑯ Adam and Eve; ⑰ the angels foretelling Isaac's birth to Abraham; ⑱ St. Michael fighting the dragon; ⑲ Abraham preparing to sacrifice Isaac; ⑳ Jacob's dream of the ladder.

On the lower level of the left window are New Testament figures associated with the Good News (Gospel): ㉑ an angel foretelling John the Baptist's birth to Zacharias; ㉒ the Annunciation to the Blessed Virgin Mary; ㉓ St. Gabriel with lilies of the Annunciation; ㉔ angels visiting the shepherds; ㉕ the angel foretelling the birth of Christ to Joseph.

In **the right, or eastern, window** are scenes from the Acts of the Apostles, featuring primarily St. Peter and St. Paul: ㉖ St. Peter preaching; ㉗ St. Peter healing the lame man; ㉘ St. Peter with the keys to the Kingdom; ㉙ the stoning of Stephen; ㉚ St. Philip baptizing the eunuch; ㉛ St. Peter raising Tabitha; ㉜ the conversion of St. Paul's jailer; ㉝ St. Paul with a sword; ㉞ St. Paul laying hands on St. Timothy; ㉟ St. Titus and St. Paul before Festus.

Other Features

• All of the chapel windows were made by C. E. Kempe and Company of London.

• In the two high niches of the south wall are statues of St. Eric IX, king of Sweden (left), and Canute the Great, king of England, Denmark, and Norway (right); and in the niche at the west end of the north aisle is the figure of St. Eskill, bishop and martyr.

• On the ambulatory side of the entrance bay are two statues: St. John the Baptist (above) and St. Ansgar with a pastoral staff and miter holding a small cathedral. Both sculptures are by John Evans of Boston.

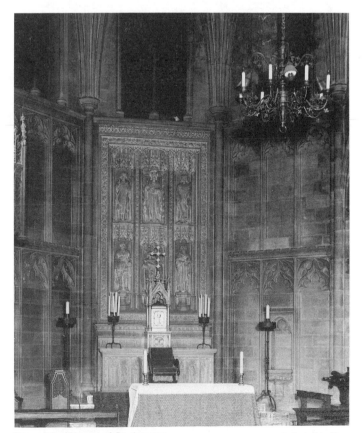

Altar of the Chapel of St. Ansgar   Cathedral Archives

Stone carved font in Baptistry

The Baptistry and Columbarium

t the northeast corner of the crossing are five steps rising to the ambulatory (the aisle or walkway that curves around the choir and altar in the style of medieval French cathedrals).

Beyond those steps and to the left is a three-chambered complex comprising the baptistry and the columbarium. This unit, designed by Cram and Ferguson, was the gift of the descendants of Peter Stuyvesant (1592–1682), the last Dutch governor of what was then the New Netherlands. The baptistry is heralded by a handsome bronze grille/screen, which gives access to the outer chamber or entrance way. On a smaller scale, this foyer serves the pilgrim in the same manner as the narthex at the western end of the Cathedral: it sharpens the focus in preparation for a more specialized experience.

Over the screen gateway are the words, "Behold the Lamb which taketh away the sins of the world" (John 1:29). Lower and to the left is engraved "We bless Thy Holy Name for Thy servant Catherine E. S. Stuyvesant, departed this life in faith and fear, 1924."

Above **the arch** leading from the entrance foyer into the baptistry is ① the coat of arms of the Netherlands. To the left ② is a statue of St. Catherine of Alexandria (fourth century), beneath which is a bladed wheel, the symbol of her torture. To the right ③ is St. Nicholas (also fourth century). Below his statue are the three purses of gold that he allegedly gave to a poor man so that his daughters might be supported and saved from lives of prostitution. (This legend is the origin of the three gold balls that constitute the insignia of a pawnbroker.) All of the statuary in this archway is the work of W. F. Ross and Company.

On the east (right) wall of **the entrance way** is ④ a statue of Judith Bayard, wife of Peter Stuyvesant; and under it ⑤ is a bust of the donor's father, August Van Horne Stuyvesant, as a child. Across on the west wall of this foyer ⑥ is the figure of Louise de Coligny, the wife of William of Orange. Beneath is ⑦ a bust of the donor's mother, Harriet LeRoy Stuyvesant as a child, created by Randolph Rogers in 1844.

Entrance into **the main chamber** brings two striking perceptions: the dominance of the octagonal form and the great sense of upward thrust. Baptistries are traditionally octagonal, dating back to a patristic rationale. Since God had saved eight human beings *from* water in Noah's Ark, the space in which God's children are saved *by* water should be eight-sided.

In a room thirty-one feet in diameter, a true sense of uplift is conveyed by vaulting, which extends forty-three feet from the floor, plus a crowning lantern the apex of which extends fourteen feet higher still. Not visible from indoors, but adding to the verticality of this structure, is the external finial, which reaches a height of eighty feet. Ralph Adams Cram, in open admiration of his colleague Frank Cleveland, who conceived of the Portuguese-style interlacing of ribs from the eight corners of the structure, speculated on adapting this principle to the larger challenge of the crown of the Cathedral's crossing.

In the center of the baptistry, raised three steps above the floor, is a **font** ⑧, a monumental structure of Champville marble fifteen feet in height. From the center of the bowl rises an octagonal pinnacled shaft with several strata of art deco carvings. One can imagine the tension for sculptor Albert H. Atkins as he neared completion of this undertaking, anxious that no mistake spoil his masterpiece.

On the lower level are the coat of arms of the City of New York, the Diocese of New York, the Cathedral, and the Stuyvesant family. Above are the four Evangelists flanked by angels singing, praying, playing a lyre, and bearing a censer. Still higher are eight figures and symbols commemorating certain Joyful and Sorrowful Mysteries: the Annunciation (lily), the Nativity (star), the Baptism (shell), the Last Supper (chalice), the Mocking (thorns), the Crucifixion (three nails), the Resurrection (I.H.S.), and the Ascension (dove). Above all, surmounting the finial, is the figure of Christ as a youth.

More clearly visible in detail are the eight scenes and eight figures surrounding **the base of the font:** 9 the Angel of Annunciation with a lily; 10 the heavenly messenger prophesying the birth of St. John to his father, Zacharias; 11 the Angel of Sorrow with a cross symbolizing the martyrdom of Christ and St. John the Baptist; 12 the Visitation of the Virgin Mary to St. Elizabeth (mother of St. John the Baptist) with St. Mary uttering the Magnificat; 13 the Recording Angel with pen and ink; 14 Zacharias naming the infant "John"; 15 a Guardian Angel praying; 16 St. John the Baptist in the wilderness, called to preach and baptize; 17 the Angel of Sacrifice with a palm; 18 St. John the Baptist

preaching; 19 the Angel of Baptism with a shell; 20 St. John the Baptist baptizing Jesus in the River Jordan; 21 the Angel of Testimony with a scroll; 22 Jesus testifying to John the Baptist's mission; 23 the Angel of Death hooded; 24 St. John the Baptist's martyrdom.

Just as each of the nearby apsidal chapels is identified with a particular nationality of European immigrants to the United States, the baptistry honors the Dutch. On its eight walls is a **frieze** with a sculpture of six famous Netherlanders plus Britishers Henry Hudson (who was sailing under Dutch commission when he explored the Hudson River) and Henry Compton (named first rector of Trinity Church by William III, who had been prince of Orange). Visitors who have become accustomed to the latter-day purity of unadorned statuary may be surprised that these statues, the work of the renowned John Angel, are polychromed in the manner of most classical and medieval sculpture. Each statue is flanked by the symbolic shields of two saints as follows:

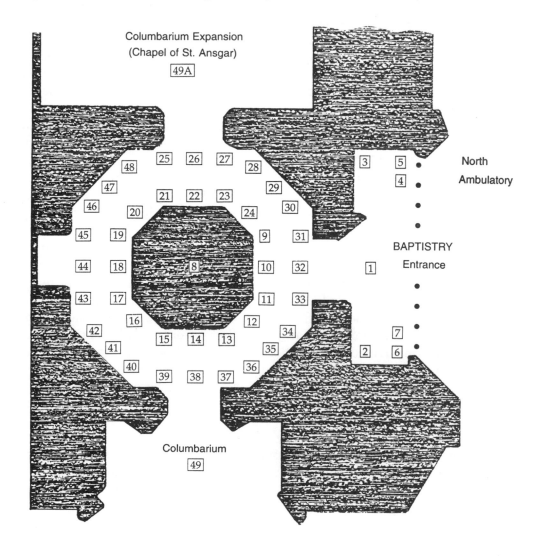

Detail in baptismal font

SHIELDS	STATUES	SHIELDS
25 Keys St. Peter	26 Henry Compton bishop of London (1632–1713)	27 Eagle St. John
28 Scallop Shells St. James	29 St. Willibrord Apostle of Frisians (648–739)	30 Diagonal Cross St. Andrew
31 Basket of Leaves St. Philip	32 Thomas à Kempis ascetic scholar (1379–1471)	33 Spears St. Thomas
34 Knives St. Bartholomew	35 Erasmus scholar and teacher (1467–1536)	36 Angel St. Matthew
37 Fuller's Clubs St. James Minor	38 Hugo Grotius jurist and scholar (1583–1645)	39 Fishes St. Simon
40 Ship St. Jude	41 William of Orange liberator of the Netherlands (1533–84)	42 Axes St. Matthias
43 Swords St. Paul	44 Henry Hudson explorer (died 1611)	45 Tongues of Fire St. Barnabas
46 Lion St. Mark	47 Peter Stuyvesant director general of New Netherlands (1592–1682)	48 Ox St. Luke

The Columbarium

Outsiders might think it strange, or even depressing, that the baptistry would be closely connected to the columbarium, in which the ashes of the deceased repose. From a Christian perspective, however, it is eminently appropriate.

The columbarium is a latter-day urban version of God's Acre, the burial ground surrounding the parish church in the days of our ancestors. It is a reminder of our mortality and the larger context within which our earthly life and death are placed by the Crucifixion and Resurrection.

Started in the 1970s in the alcove 49 at the west end of the baptistry, it has since expanded to the east 49A into St. Ansgar's Chapel.

Each vault is constructed entirely of marble and becomes one with the walls of the Cathedral, enshrined in the most permanent dignity this world knows. Thus do the ashes of the dead adjoin the living in worship, even as the souls of the righteous join in the timeless praise of Almighty God. Burial in the Cathedral's columbarium is open to all people.

Choir, Sanctuary, and Presbytery

The Choir, Sanctuary, and Presbytery

There is no consistent or official nomenclature for the climactic portion of the Cathedral bordered by the crossing and the ambulatory. Some authorities use "choir" for the entire area; others designate the portion surrounding the high altar as "sanctuary." Another refinement distinguishes the space occupied by clergy and celebrants (presbyters) as "presbytery." To complicate matters further, the term "chancel" is often used (though not at St. John's) to apply to any or all of the foregoing.

Because the entire space at St. John's is bound together in a crescendo of magnificence based on the vision described in the Revelation of St. John the Divine, we will look briefly at the area as a whole, standing at the east end of the crossing, before considering its component parts.

Richness of color seems everywhere evident, starting with the green Pennsylvania marble treads and the yellow Numidian risers leading up to the first level (the choir proper). Beyond, the steps to the presbytery are of pink marble from Hauteville, France. At the base of the choir piers is a broad course of red jasper (Rev. 4:3) surmounted by a green molding of Pennsylvania serpentine. Transcendent colors from the major windows above (see "The Eastern Clerestory Windows," pp. 133–136) provide a crowning brilliance. In the center of this radiance is the white marble altar symbolizing the Lamb of God. Thus does the eastern end of the Cathedral reach its climax in the manner of Revelation 4, 5, and 6, where, amid the splendor of thrones and lightning and torches and elders and angels comes the affirmation, "Worthy is the Lamb who was slain."

Through the Romanesque arches behind the high altar can be seen a raw brick wall which will acquire a revetment of white marble, reinforcing this sense of purity at the heart of the surrounding grandeur. It is the only portion of the eastern end of the Cathedral that awaits completion.

The Choir

The Choir Stalls, rising in three tiers on either side, were made by John Barber Company, Philadelphia, following the design of Heins and LaFarge. Made of oak, their style was influenced by the stalls of San Domenica Cathedral, Taormina, Sicily. The carved finials of the uppermost stalls present the figures of musicians and composers of sacred music. On the south side, from right to left are:

• David, king of Israel in the eleventh century B.C.E., a harp player credited with the *Book of Psalms;* • St. Cecilia, second century C.E., Roman maiden and martyr, patron of sacred music. • Giovanni Palestrina, Italian composer (1524–94); • Henry Purcell, English prodigy who at age eighteen was appointed organist at Westminster Abbey (1658–95); • Franz Joseph Haydn, Austrian composer (1732–1809); • Felix Mendelssohn, German composer (1809–47).

On the north side, from left to right are:

• St. Gregory the Great, pope, writer, liturgist, and musician (Gregorian chant, 540–604); • Thomas Tallis, considered the father of English Cathedral music (1515–85); • Johann Sebastian Bach, German organist and composer (1685–1750); • George Frederick Handel, German-born resident of England, composer (1685–1759); • Dimitri Bortniansky, composer, systematizer of Russian church music (1752–1825).

[127]

South bank of hand-carved choir stalls

The Compass Rose is set in the pavement center of the Great Choir. It is the official emblem of the Worldwide Anglican Communion, of which the Episcopal Church of America is part.

At its core is the Cross of St. George, traditional symbol of the Celtic Christianity, which originally gave the leadership that brought the Anglican Church into being. This shield is surrounded by a circular band bearing the New Testament teaching, written in Greek. "The truth shall make you free." Radiating from this band are the compass points, symbolic of the universality of the Anglican Communion. Surmounting the shield is a miter, time-honored symbol of the Apostolic Order.

Originally designed by the late Canon Edward N. West in 1954 for the first Anglican Congress ever held in the United States (Minneapolis), the Cathedral's Compass Rose was dedicated as a memorial to him on September 20, 1992, and blessed by the Most Reverend George Carey, 103rd archbishop of Canterbury, whose cathedral in England had installed its own Compass Rose following the Lambeth Conference in 1989.

John Barton, architect in residence, honored Canon West's original size and color design in this rendition set in variegated marble and brass. It also marks the final resting place of the canon's ashes.

The Dean's Stall is at the western end of the south bank of choir stalls. Designed by Cram and Ferguson, it was made by Irving and Casson of Boston and was the gift of the Head Mistresses' Association in memory of Agnes Irwin, 1841–1914, first dean of Radcliffe College.

The Pipe Organ console, which controls the 141 ranks of 8,035 pipes of the Aeolian-Skinner instrument, is located above the middle of the south bank of choir stalls. It consists of four manual keyboards plus pedals. Because there will eventually be 17 million cubic feet of space to fill, this is one of the loudest pipe organs in existence. However, it is by no means the largest. Even within New York City there are several instruments with more pipes (Riverside Church, St. Bartholemew's Episcopal Church, St. Thomas Episcopal Church, St. Patrick's Catholic Cathedral).

The largest pipe organ ever constructed (33,212 pipes) is in the Convention Hall in Atlantic City, N.J.; but many of its ranks have fallen into desuetude. The largest functioning pipe organ (30,067 pipes) is at Wanamaker's department store in Philadelphia. Beyond a certain point, however, size becomes of lesser importance than setting and acoustics as far as satisfaction or inspiration for the listener is concerned. From an aural and emotional standpoint, the ambience of a department store, with the music wafting over the lingerie and men's wear, is very different from that when it resounds and echoes through a great Gothic or Romanesque church.

The original pipe organ at St. John's was built by the firm of Ernest M. Skinner in 1910. The opening of the nave in 1941 brought a need for an extensive rebuilding of that instrument, a project deferred by World War II and not completed until 1954. To correct an imbalance in which some of the deep notes from the thirty-two-foot pipes were drowning out treble sounds, many of the smaller pipes were doubled. The majority of the organ pipes are positioned high in the enlarged triforium chambers north and south of the choir in ranks of sixty-one pipes (five chromatic octaves per stop). However, the most commanding rank of all, called the State Trumpet, is located beneath the western rose window, five hundred feet from the console and the other organ pipes, necessitating careful timing by the organist.

The Sanctuary and Presbytery

The focal point in most Christian churches is the principal, or high, altar. Following the Reformation, many Protestant churches, in an effort to place prime emphasis on Scripture, put the pulpit in that raised central spot with the Bible resting upon it. However, the trend in the late twentieth century has been to return to a combination of pulpit and lectern, which are positioned on opposite sides of the altar.

At St. John the Divine, as in other churches in the liturgical tradition, the area including and surrounding the high altar is called "the sanctuary." It is the *sanctum sanctorum* (called "holy of holies" in the Jewish temple).

Close by the sanctuary, and considered an extension of it, is the presbytery, where officiating clergy are seated. The presbytery was anciently located in a semicircle behind the high altar. At St. John's it is between the high altar and the choir. The best vantage point from which to behold this entire area, surely the climactic part of the church, is the north/south passageway east of the choir. The following descriptions are written from that view:

1️⃣ **The Cathedra** is the bishop's seat, or throne. It comes from the Greek word for "chair." Its presence names a church "cathedral." When a bishop makes a formal pronouncement, it is called *ex cathedra* (from the seat of authority). This cathedra was carved by

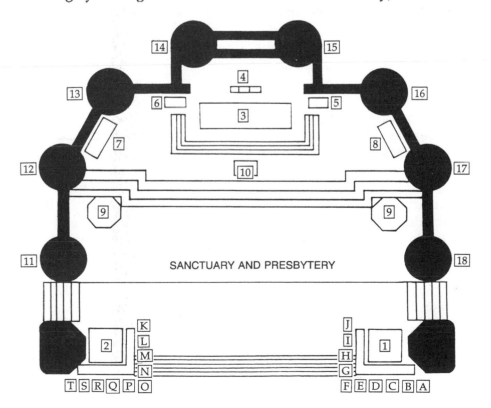

SANCTUARY AND PRESBYTERY

the John Barber Company from plans by Heins and LaFarge.

Above the seat is the diocesan coat of arms, which includes a miter (bishop's hat), a key (symbol of bishops dating back to St. Peter), and a staff (representing the bishop's role as shepherd). The coat of arms below contains an eagle (symbol of the United States), crossed swords (from the coat of arms of the bishop of London, under whose jurisdiction the American colonial church first came), and two windmills (from the coat of arms of New Amsterdam, New York City's first name). Matching the cathedra on the north side is ② **the International/Ecumenical Cathedra** for the primates and archbishops of the worldwide Anglican Communion and for visiting church leaders. The other cathedral known to have two cathedras is the National Cathedral in Washington, D.C., one for the bishop of Washington and one for the presiding bishop of the Episcopal Church of America.

③ **The High Altar** is a free-standing mensa of white Vermont marble. It bears the inscription "To the glory of God and in memory of Anna Livingston Morton, 1846–1918." Above the high altar is ④ **The Great Cross,** made of wood polychromed in the manner of the twelfth century. The figure of Christ Triumphant, commonly used in the devotions of the early church instead of Christ Crucified, was carved by Cornelia van Auken Chapin. The research and polychroming were carried out by Roswell Forman Barratt and Canon Edward Nason West.

⑤ **The Magna Carta Pedestal** is to the right of the altar. It is supported by a shaft made of three stones from the ruins of the altar of the ancient Abbey of Bury St. Edmunds, England. It was there that the barons swore before the altar to secure from King John the liberties embodied in the Magna Carta. Made of Caen stone, these were given to the Cathedral in 1922, with the consent of the abbey authorities, by the Marquess of Bristol with assistance from Dr. Raphael Constantin of New York. Upon this pedestal and ⑥ a matching replica at the left of the high altar are ⑦ two cloisonné imperial **Shinto vases** given to the Cathedral by Emperor Hirohito of Japan in 1926, the first year of his reign.

On the left side of the sanctuary is ⑧ **the Pontifical Sedile,** where the bishop sits when he is celebrating the liturgy. The adorning needlepoint is the work and gift of Mrs. William Warner Hoppin. The back of the seat displays the coat of arms of the

Diocese of New York. The icon above the sedile was the gift of the metropolitan of Odessa, Russia. In a corresponding position on the right are 8A **Sedilia for other clergy** (priests and deacons).

Among the most unusual appointments in the entire church are ⑨ **the Menorah,** which stand on both sides of the high altar. Massive, seven-branched candlesticks, each weighing more than a ton, they are made of bronze overlaid with gold and stand on bases of Lavanda marble. They were designed after those used in Solomon's Temple, as portrayed on the Arch of Titus in Rome. They were given to the Cathedral in 1926 by Adolph Ochs, publisher of the *New York Times.* At their dedication, Bishop Manning noted "They will be to us a symbol of the relation between the Old and New Testaments, and will portray the debt owed by Christianity to Judaism."

Beneath the antique Bijart rug that leads from the floor of the Great Choir to the high altar is ⑩ **the Ephesus Tile** from the Church of St. John the Divine in Ephesus, built under direction of the sixth-century Emperor Justinian over the traditional site of St. John's grave.

The Eight Granite Columns, which curve around the eastern portion of the sanctuary are, for many, the most unusual physical feature of the entire building. Quarried as monoliths from Bear Island, near Vinal Haven, Maine, they are 55 feet in height (not counting the capital, which is of a different stone), 6 feet in diameter, and weigh 130 tons each. Problems in the polishing required that they each be cut into two pieces (the line of demarcation can barely be seen on some of them). How much easier the quarrying would have been had this been known in advance. Transported by tug-powered barges to a dock on 134th Street, they were then winched by steam tractor to the Cathedral site. Later it was discovered that every manhole cover that they had crossed had broken.

The foundation of these columns goes 135 feet to bedrock. They were quarried by John Pierce of Vinal Haven, Maine, and were given as memorials to the people whose names are carved on the bases of the columns as seen on the ambulatory side. Reading from north to south:

⑪ Joseph Lawrence, 1788–1872, given by Sebastian D. Lawrence; ⑫ Josiah Mason Fiske, 1823–92, given by Mrs. George W. Collard; ⑬ John Divine Jones, 1814–95, given by Mrs. Josephine K. Jones; ⑭ John Jacob Astor, 1763–1848, given by Colonel

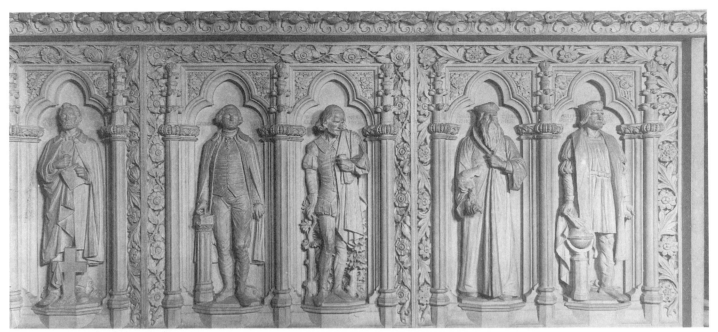

Northern end of Historical Parapet

John Jacob Astor; 15 Eugene Augustus Hoffman, 1829–1902, given by the family of Dean Hoffman; 16 Harry Manigault Morris, 1817–92, given by Georgia E. Morris; 17 Colonel Richard Tylden Auchmuty, U.S.V., 1831–93, given by Mrs. Ellen S. Auchmuty; 18 Alonzo Potter, Bishop of Pennsylvania, 1800–1865, given by Bishop Henry C. Potter.

The Seven Sanctuary Lamps, directly over the walkway, symbolize the Seven Gifts of the Holy Spirit (Isa. 11:2) and the seven candles before the altar of God (Rev. 1:12–20). Modeled after an ancient lamp in the Holy Sepulchre, Jerusalem, they are pewter-covered brass, measuring nine feet from bottom ring to counterweight. They are memorials to James and Mary Green, given by their children.

The Sanctuary Arch, which separates the eastern end of the church from the choir, is inscribed: "This sanctuary arch is given to the glory of God and in grateful memory of the life and work of David Hummell Greer, eighth bishop of New York."

The Historical Parapet, at the ascent to the presbytery, is designed to present outstanding characters from each of the first twenty centuries of the Christian era. Originally its form was linear, from south to north. Now its two sections enclose the bishop's seat (on the south side) and the suffragan bishops' stalls (on the north). It is built mainly of Champville (France) marble. The statues read chronologically from right to left (authorities differ slightly on a few of the dates given): A St. Paul (died 66 C.E.) with a sword symbolizing his manner of death; B St. Justin Martyr (100–165) with an axe and block; C St. Clement of Alexandria (150–220) holding a cross in his left hand; D St. Athanasius (296–373) pouring baptismal water from a seashell; E St. Augustine of Hippo (354–430) with miter, pen, and tablet; F St. Benedict (480–543) in the habit of a Benedictine monk; G St. Gregory the Great (550–604) with a slave child in broken shackles; H Charles Martel (688–741) with a crown, battle-axe, and pennant; I Charlemagne (742–814) with crown, scepter, and orb; J Alfred the Great (849–901) crowned, with a sword by his side; K Godfrey de Bouillon (1061–1100) with a Crusader's sword and shield; L St. Bernard (1091–1153) holding a cross and a book; M St. Francis of Assisi (1182–1226) in Franciscan habit; N John Wycliffe (1325–84) with book and staff; O Christopher Columbus (1436–1506) lifting a veil from the globe; P Archbishop Thomas Cranmer (1489–1556) thrusting his hand into a flame; Q William Shakespeare (1564–1616) standing amid laurels; R George Washington (1732–99) in civilian attire as president; S Abraham Lincoln (1809–65) delivering the Gettysburg Address; T An empty niche, beneath which is an uncarved block. This awaits the end of the twentieth century (and the second millennium) and has been the source of great interest and speculation as to who is waiting to be released from that stone and placed in the existing pantheon.

Commentary

A Noise That Is More Than Joyful

It would be anticlimactic if a great church with outstanding visual art did not have music that reinforced the sense of magnificence and the feeling of uplift conveyed by arches, sculpture, and stained-glass windows. From the outset, the leadership at St. John's has striven for excellence in music. As in other areas of liturgy, the best of tradition has been retained but new forms of expression are also used.

The liturgical music is based on three established traditions: Jewish, pre-Reformation Christian, and Anglican. This may be the only cathedral in which the main Sunday service (11:00 A.M.) includes the following intonation by cantor and worshipers:

Omega Liturgical Dancers   Mary Bloom

Baba Olatunji and Ensemble welcome Archbishop Tutu   Mary Bloom

*"Sh'ma Yisrael Adonai Elohaynu Adonai Echad.
Hear, O Israel, the Lord our God is one Lord."*

The chanting of one of the three-thousand-year-old Psalms is also an integral part of the early portion of the service leading to the Eucharist.

Subsequent movements of the liturgy — Kyrie, Gloria, Credo, Sanctus, Agnus Dei, and Benedictus — retain their Latin or Greek designations and are often chanted in Latin. The same is true of the canticles included in Sunday Vespers (7:00 P.M.).

The choirs are based on the English cathedral choir system with one notable exception. Since 1975, St. John's choirs have been the only cathedral choirs to include women and girls. The Choristers (boys and girls from fifth to eighth grades) are drawn from the Cathedral School. The professional choir is made up primarily of free-lance musicians, who may also sing in synagogues on Fridays and Saturdays. The Volunteer Choir consists of approximately twenty-five men and women who participate two Sundays per month as well as on feast days.

Two innovative and popular musical settings for the standard words of the liturgy have premiered at the Cathedral. Duke Ellington, who was a member of the congregation and was buried from the Cathedral, presented his first Sacred Concert here. The Paul Winter Consort, longtime resident artists, have presented the Missa Gaia (Earth Mass) regularly on the first Sunday of October, when the feast of St. Francis is celebrated.

The Eastern Clerestory Windows

wo sets of clerestory windows curve around the eastern end of the Cathedral above the choir and sanctuary. The lower seven, called ambulatory clerestories, constitute a major feature of the church building, especially when their brilliance is highlighted by the morning sun. Above them are five smaller windows, the sanctuary clerestories.

Sanctuary Clerestories

The central figure Ⅰ is a mature St. Paul in the tonsured hair style that has become his identifying attribute. On either side are two archangels, each holding a symbol of one of the four Evangelists. Those are not easily identifiable to the naked eye: Ⅱ St. Matthew (angel), Ⅲ St. Mark (winged lion), Ⅳ St. Luke (winged ox), and Ⅴ St. John (eagle). Made by Wilbur Herbert Burnham of Boston, these windows honor John Henry Hobart, third bishop of New York and seventh rector of Trinity Parish.

Ambulatory Clerestories

The sheer beauty of these windows requires no background knowledge for enjoyment. But if one is to understand their meaning and symbolism, it might be helpful to review "St. John and the Revelation" (pp. 17–18) or undertake more extensive study of the last book of the Bible.

Made of glass stained with deep, glowing colors of the pre-Raphaelite style by James Powell and Sons of London, each window is twenty-eight feet high and seventeen feet wide.

The rosettes at the tops of these seven ambulatory clerestories symbolize the message of St. John the Divine to the seven churches in Asia as recorded in the book of Revelation. They are designed to be read from left (north) to right (south).

St. John and the Seven Churches

The leftmost window (above the entrance to the Chapel of St. Ansgar) is identified with ① the church at Ephesus. This window also sets the theme for all of the ambulatory clerestories by including references to each of the seven Asian churches in the panels (lancets) below. In the top of the center panel 1A St. John is depicted between two praying angels holding the cup that is one of his symbols. Below, 1B he appears as the aged exile on the Isle of Patmos, sitting with book in lap and pen in hand and listening to the words of the angel behind him. In the side panels are the angels of the seven churches bearing on scrolls their names: 1C Ephesus, 1D Smyrna and Pergamos, 1E Thyatira and Sardis, 1F Philadelphia and Laodicea.

The window was given by Mrs. E. D. Ludlow Johnson in memory of Gabriel Ludlow. It is best viewed from the eastern entrance to St. James Chapel on an early summer morning.

The Natural Elements

The second window from the left, above St. Boniface Chapel, is identified with ② the church at Smyrna and features the natural elements upon which the vials of God's wrath were poured (Rev. 16). In the lower left panel 2A an angel holds the earth; in the middle 2B three angels hold the air (invisible), the sun (yellow-green), and the sea (green waves). To the right 2C an angel holds the rivers and fountains (blue currents).

In the upper middle 2D is the Lamb that was slain, with symbols of the Evangelists on either side: 2E the lion and the man-faced beast; 2F the ox and the eagle.

The window is given in memory of Anne Ellen Wallace.

[133]

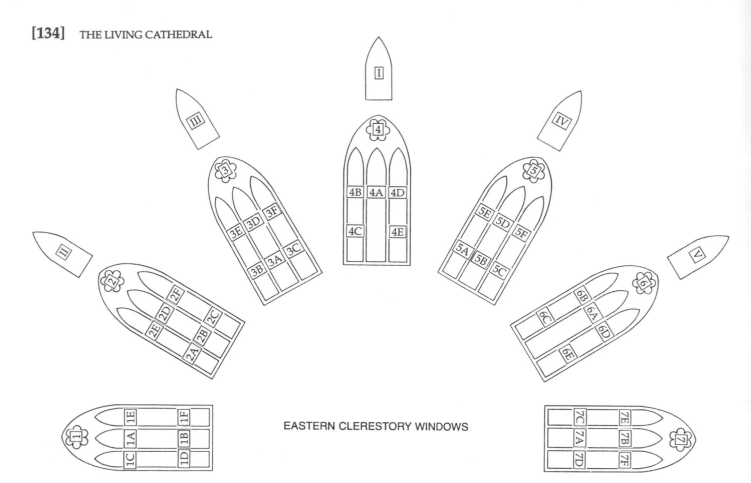

EASTERN CLERESTORY WINDOWS

The Seven Angels with Trumpets

Third from the left, rising above St. Columba Chapel, is a window whose rosette ③ identifies the church at Pergamos. The lancets below are based on Revelation 8:2.

Three angels 3A are in the lower part of the middle lancet with two more on each side 3B , 3C . In the upper middle 3D is the angel with the cloud overarched by the rainbow standing upon the sea. To the left 3E is the angel with the seal of the living God and to the right 3F is the angel with the golden censer. In the central part of the two side lancets are four angels (two on each side) blowing the four winds of the earth.

The window was given by Josephine Eliza Leeds in memory of John William Leeds, Eliza Leeds, and Emily Irene Hardenbergh.

Christ Reigning in Glory

The central and dominating window of the ambulatory is above St. Savior Chapel. The rosette ④ symbolizes the church at Thyatira. But the major theme is the reigning Christ as described in the first chapter of Revelation. The window was given in memory of Whitelaw Reed.

In the middle panel, garbed in dazzling red 4A is the son of man vested as King and Priest. (On certain mornings in late spring and early summer, the sunlight passing through this lancet gives a molten brilliance to the bronze doors six hundred feet away). He is wearing a royal crown and a golden pallium and stands amid seven candlesticks, holding in his right hand seven stars. (The Cathedral's coat of arms, shown in the center of the diagram, is based on the Scripture passage here depicted: Revelation 1:12–16.)

Beneath the reigning Christ a rainbow overarches a sea of glass. In the side panels are the principal archangels: 4B St. Michael in armor is shown as prince of celestial armies. The balance in his left hand is for the weighing of souls and symbolizes his role as Guardian Angel of Departed Spirits. Below 4C St. Raphael, with pilgrim staff is shown as the friendly traveler (Milton's "affable archangel"). At the top of the right lancet is 4D St. Gabriel as Angel of Annunciation; below 4E is St. Uriel as Angel of Light holding the sun.

The Seven Last Plagues

The theme of the window over the entrance to St. Martin's Chapel (third from the right) is taken from Revelation 15, which is a climactic echo to the plagues in the Old Testament book of Exodus.

In the rosette 5 are symbols of the church of Sardis. At the lower level of the three lancets are 5A two angels, 5B three angels, and 5C two angels, a total of seven holding seven vials (Rev. 15:1). In the upper part of the middle lancet 5D an angel holds aloft the Gospel as a scroll; on the upper left 5E is an angel with a measuring rod; in the right 5F an angel in the sun (not to be confused with the Woman in the Sun featured in the next window).

The window was given in memory of Sophia R. C. Furniss and Mary B. Hubber.

The Woman in the Sun

The second window from the right, high above St. Ambrose Chapel, has in its rosette 6 a symbol of the church of Philadelphia in Asia. The outstanding scene, filling the center lancet, is 6A the woman clothed in the sun. Based on Revelation 12:1–17, she is shown surrounded by flaming rays. Above, a cloud of glory carries her child to the throne of God. In the top of the left panel 6B is an angel proclaiming the fall of Babylon (a code name for Rome in this Scripture passage); and below, symbolizing that wicked city, is 6C the woman in scarlet holding the cup of abominations and seated on the beast from the bottomless pit.

On the top right 6D is the angel with the sharp sickle and cluster of vine; below 6E the angel with the keys to the bottomless pit and the chain to bind the dragon. The Woman in the Sun represents the Virgin Mary and the message repeats that of the central window: God triumphs over the forces of evil.

The window was given in memory of Morgan Lewis Livingstone and Catharine Manning Livingstone by their daughter Julia Livingstone.

The Heavenly City

The final or rightmost of this set of clerestories is above the eastern entrance to St. James Chapel. The church alluded to in the rosette 7 is Laodicea.

The reference is Revelation 21 and 22, the final words of Christian Scripture. In the lower middle panel is 7A an angel showing the Heavenly City; and above 7B is a glorified figure symbolizing that city, the New Jerusalem, coming down from heaven.

In the lower left panel 7C is an angel with the Alpha, balanced on the right by 7D an angel with the Omega. (These are the first and last letters of the Greek alphabet. They appear in Revelation 1, 21, and 22 in the same proclamation, "I am the Alpha and the Omega, the beginning and the end.") Above each 7E, 7F is an angel beckoning and saying "Come."

The Woman in the Sun – Ambulatory Clerestory   Cathedral Archives

Exhibit Hall – viewed from Diocesan House

A. Hansen

Appendix

Bronze casting of sculpture by school child – Peace Fountain

G. Lynas

Adoration of the Magi – Tapestry in the Crossing

A. L. Gustafson

Tapestries

Foremost among the Cathedral's moveable art treasures are forty Renaissance tapestries. The collection is unrivaled among the churches of the world. Half of these hang in the main worship area and are identified below. Less sturdy than the stone that surrounds them, these huge hangings are vulnerable to light, dust, and dryness. Moreover, their own weight tends to pull them apart.

Restoration is a never-ending need. Hence the formation of the Cathedral's own textile restoration program. Started in the early 1980s, it has attracted top professionals who welcome a chance to take a stitch in time. By the 1990s there were seven people in the program. However, the need to generate their own support has caused this team to accept outside assignments. Works of art in need of professional attention come in from throughout the nation; so the Cathedral's tapestries must take their place in line.

Barberini Collection

When all of them are in place, there are twelve Barberini tapestries at the crossing, six each at the entrances to what will one day be the north and south transepts. The cartoons came from the mind and hand of Giovanni Francesco Romanelli, who at an early age won the patronage of the powerful Cardinal Barberini, whose uncle was Pope Urban VIII.

The twelve "Scenes in the Life and Death of Christ" were commissioned by the cardinal and woven on the papal loom by Jacques de la Rivière. Just as they were being completed, Pope Urban VIII died, ending the cardinal's access to the throne and putting his life in some danger.

Barberini fled to France, taking his protégé and the tapestries with him. They were never exhibited at the Vatican and have never been reproduced. Romanelli's talents were recognized in Paris and his various works exhibited at the Louvre. His name at this point became Jean François Romanelli, and it is as such that it has been recorded in subsequent history.

In the nineteenth century these tapestries, which had become identified with the cardinal's name, came to the Ffoulke Collection in Washington, D.C. And in 1891 Elizabeth U. Coles presented the Barberini tapestries to the Cathedral of St. John the Divine.

This was an extraordinary act of faith, since the Cathedral was still one year short of a cornerstone. That faith has been rewarded in an unusual way. No one could have predicted that the construction would spurt at the outset and continue until the presbytery, choir, and crossing were enclosed. After that, there was a suspension of activity for two world wars and an additional hiatus of thirty years after World War II before construction was resumed at a more measured pace.

The upshot is that Mrs. Coles's priceless gifts have had, and will continue to have, a position of rare prominence at the crux of the church, where thousands of worshipers see them each week. What other repository of classic religious art has two exhibition spaces, each of which is 120 feet high and 100 feet wide?

Mortlake Collection

Eight of the tapestries in the nave are a set entitled "The Acts of the Apostles." Pope Leo X commissioned Raphael to draw the cartoons in 1513. After several sets had been completed by Belgian weavers, the cartoons were lost. Rediscovered in the seventeenth century, they were used to create a dozen new sets by the Mortlake weavers in England. The papal depictions in the original borders were changed to floral and cherubic patterns. The Cathedral's set is the gift of Mary Louise Brugiere.

In the Crossing

A Adoration of the Magi (Matt. 2:1–12); B the Last Supper (John 13:1–30; also in Matthew, Mark, and Luke); C the Resurrection (Matt. 28:1–20; also in Mark, Luke, and John); D the Transfiguration (Matt. 17:1–14; also in Mark and Luke); E Peter receiving the keys to the Kingdom (Matt. 16:13–20); F the Agony at the Mount of Olives (Matt. 26:36–46; also in Mark, Luke, and John); G the Crucifixion (Matt. 27:33–56; also in Mark, Luke, and John); H map of the Holy Land; I Baptism of Jesus (Mark 1:9–11; also in Matthew and Luke); J the Annunciation (Luke 1:26–38); K the Flight into Egypt (Matt. 2:13–18); L the Adoration of the Shepherds (Luke 2:8–14).

In the Nave

1 The Death of Ananias (Acts 5:1–11); 2 Healing of the Lame Man (John 5:2–9); 3 Miraculous Draught of Fishes (Luke 5:1–11); 4 Christ's Charge to Peter — "Feed my sheep" (John 21:16); 5 Paul Preaching at Athens (Acts 17:16–34); 6 the Sacrifice at Lystra (Acts 14:8–18); 7 the Blinding of Elymas in the Court of Sergius Paulus (Acts 13:6–12); 8 the Death of Sapphira (Acts 5:1–11); 9 King Joash of Judah Reading the Law (2 Kings 12:1–17; also in 2 Chronicles). Although not part of the Mortlake Collection, this tapestry, woven in Antwerp, Belgium, is also the gift of Mary Louise Brugiere. It is the only Old Testament portrayal in the Cathedral's tapestry collection.

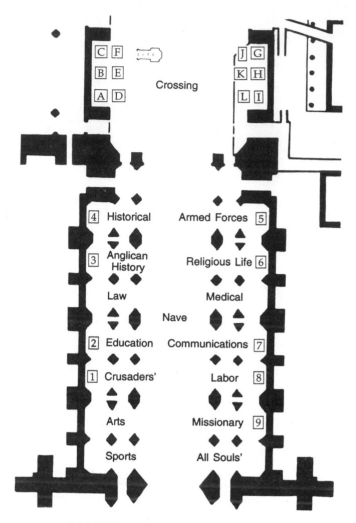

LOCATION OF HANGING TAPESTRIES

 *Commentary*

Warps and Wefts

"Warp and woof" is the archaic term for those strands, interwoven at right angels, that form tapestries and other fabrics. The expression lingers today as a metaphor in describing basic interdependent elements of a situation.

In weaving, "warps" continue to be the name for the taut violin strings across which the melody of design is played. But the colored woolen threads that transform craft into art are now called "wefts."

A similar evolution in terminology has changed the meaning of the word "tapestry," which has come to describe a specialized form of weaving wherein a single weft rarely extends the full length of the grid. The weft terminates wherever the artist's cartoon indicates a change of color to the weaver.

"Tapestry" was originally a broader, more generic term. Hence the renowned eleventh-century Bayeux Tapestry, which by today's definition would be classified as an embroidery.*

Tapestries have tended to appear most often in nations that are flowering culturally and economically. A woven piece was found in the tomb of King Tutankhamen, confirming the scholarship dating this art form as more than thirty-four centuries old.

---

*Whatever the nomenclature, this highly subjective but thoroughly charming portrayal of the Norman Conquest is worth a visit. Carelessly stored in the Cathedral at Bayeux for centuries, it presently has its own climate-controlled exhibit hall nearby.

Death of Ananias – Tapestry in the Nave

A. Hansen

In their heyday, Syria, Persia, and Peru each produced striking and colorful art in woven form. France and Belgium have been Europe's major fonts of this art. France supplied the enthusiasm, money, and factories whereas the Flemings have developed the greatest skills.

Some of the most celebrated tapestries of the Western world have Christian themes. The subject matter may be overt, as in the hangings of this Cathedral. The seven cardinal sins and the seven cardinal virtues have inspired famous sets of warps and wefts. In other instances, religious interpretation is readily applied to symbolic legend. The unicorn has been the central figure in two well-known sets: "The Lady and the Unicorn" in Paris's Musée de Cluny and "The Hunt of the Unicorn" in the Cloisters of New York City.

Such single-minded, labor-intensive art has subsided in an era of mass production and waning subsidies for culture and craft. Still, sagas and affirmations are occasionally expressed through handmade work of textile art in our time. Two heroic examples, both resulting form World War II, have emerged in Western Europe.

• The Warlord Embroidery, detailing the eleven months from D Day to V.E. Day, is an intentional and respectful response, nearly nine centuries later, to the Bayeux Tapestry. Together they portray the two instances, since the Roman invasion in New Testament times, of successful armed crossings of the English Channel. At eighty-three meters, Warlord is 17 percent longer than the surviving portion of the Bayeux masterpiece.

• Three-and-a-half years before the Allies invaded Normandy, during the war's darkest days, Coventry, England, experienced a massive bombing by the German Luftwaffe. Most of the inner city, including the cathedral, was destroyed by explosion and fire. Like a phoenix, a modern cathedral quickly arose near the shell of its predecessor. Behind the high altar of the new cathedral, dominating the worshiper's view, hangs the largest tapestry in the world. The size of a tennis court, Graham Sutherland's creation was woven on the Aubusson-Felletin looms in France. Its theme is "Christ of the Apocalypse" and the portrayal is as formidable, mysterious, and disturbing as its inspiration: the Revelation of St. John the Divine.

Live serpent and wary worshipers at the Feast of St. Francis celebration

God's Creatures

The earliest human markings yet discovered, on cave walls and in tombs, include representations of animals — creatures not of a lesser god but of our God. Even scientists and creationists can agree that when human beings first arrived on this spinning, orbiting sphere — whether four thousand or forty thousand years ago — there were other fauna already here as a welcoming party.

The fortunes of all God's creatures were linked in creation (Garden of Eden) and in survival (the Ark). Moreover, Scripture indicates that the finale of this terrestrial age will see a creaturely presence, whether in perfect harmony ("the wolf shall lie down with the lamb . . . the child will put his hand on the adder's den") or in apocalypse ("the beast that ascends from the bottomless pit . . . will conquer and kill them").

The serpent, first and only creature to be individually identified, was cast as a villain. Later in the Bible there are also unsympathetic references to swine, wild beasts, and dragons. The prophet Daniel foresaw the ultimate in shame for King Nebuchadnezzar as living like an animal. Hence our term "on all fours."

On the other hand, some of the tenderest moments recorded in Holy Writ involve God's other creatures. They had not only greeted Adam in the primordial mists of time, but were also upon the surrounding hillsides and by the manger itself when "the Word became flesh and dwelled among us."

And then there is the symbolism: Christ was the Lamb of God; David the Lion of Judah. Mark, Luke, and John have been depicted respectively by the winged lion, the winged ox, and the eagle, placing them on the same lofty plane as Matthew's winged human being or angel.

Double honors went to the dove, harbinger of peace in the Old Testament and figurative embodiment of the Holy Spirit in the New. Likewise the donkey, particularly revered in Israel and Spain, is associated with Mary's transport to Bethlehem and Jesus' entry into Jerusalem.

In addition to drawing upon Hebrew imagery, Christian artists have been influenced by the culture and fables of Rome, Greece, and the Orient. Thus the phoenix becomes a symbol of rebirth; the peacock is linked with immortality; the eagle with Christ's Ascension; the egg with the Resurrection. Typology has also linked the whale with the Resurrection (Jonah returned to life after three days). The pelican, piercing its own breast to feed its young, sometimes symbolizes Christ's sacrifice on the Cross. Even the serpent, properly handled, emerges as part of the symbol of healing, the caduceus.

Despite this agelong fascination with and dependency on creatures that swim, fly, slither, and walk on multiple feet, very little was done for them on an organized basis in the Western world until modern times. The veterinary profession is less than 250 years old and the societies that advocate humane treatment and animal welfare are products of the nineteenth and twentieth centuries.

Prior to 1750 the people most identified with compassion for animals were the saints. In fact, animals often helped good people become saints to the extent that the alleged ability to communicate with other species was cited as a qualifying miracle for canonization.

Most likely it was the language of love. St. Kevin is pictured with birds on his shoulders. St. Malo refused to move his cloak because a nest had been created there. Thomas Becket urged respect and care for horses. St. Jerome was reported to remove a thorn from a lion's paw.

St. Benno, annoyed by the loud croaking of nearby frogs, bade them be mute and they obeyed. Then, overcome by guilt, he released them from the spell so that they might praise God in their own way. St. Martin de Porres established a treatment center for dogs and cats and even refused to have the vermin in his clothing discommoded.

The apotheosis of animal lovers was St. Francis of Assisi, patron of all nature. Legend has him taming a fierce wolf with the sign of the Cross. Better known and authenticated was his custom of addressing with divine gaiety all creatures as "Brother": "Brother Squirrel," "Brother Ass," "Brother Sparrow."

Some would wish that the spirit of St. Francis might prevail throughout the world; but it seems improbable that true community can be achieved between species as long as one remains on the menu or in the gun sights of the other.

Meanwhile, the call of the thrush, the skylark, or the nightingale suggests a divine, terrestrial presence outside ourselves; and the faithfulness of a pet (Fido=fidelity) reminds us that humankind has not cornered the market on virtue.

෪

By design and through celebration St. John's has demonstrated an unusual sensitivity to God's creatures. The following chart indicates the various ways in which animals are portrayed in sculpture, carvings, and stained glass. Even before entering the church one is apt to see a peacock or peahen strutting about the lawns, just as similar fowls have done for centuries in the close of many a British cathedral.

The feast of St. Francis (celebrated on the first Sunday in October) may find the gigantic western doors opening to admit an elephant, a llama, a carried python, a cockatoo, and scores of pet dogs and cats. The worship has often featured the sounds of endangered species used as fugues for the liturgical music.

Such an emphasis might seem disproportionate were it not part of a larger philosophy and program that includes a range of services to endangered and disenfranchised human beings. The affection shown toward animals could seem purely sentimental were it not part of an overarching concern that includes "animals within animals," the microbes and cells without which all fauna and flora would soon perish. A strong emphasis on environment completes the Cathedral's witness to the thought that "universe," in its origins, means "one song."

Creatures at the Cathedral

Animals: General: front door, lower left portal; clerestory Sports window; clerestory Missionary window. Various: children's animal sculptures in a chain around the Peace Fountain.

Ape: Medical window.

Beehive: St. Ambrose Chapel rose window; St. Ambrose Chapel entrance screen.

Birds (general): front door, lower left portal; Creation window; clerestory Arts window; All Souls' reredos; clerestory Missionary window; Religious Life window; Motherhood rose window; Westminster medallion, clerestory ambulatory Seven Plagues window.

Calf: Fatted: clerestory Fatherhood window. Golden: clerestory Law window.

Cow: clerestory Labor window.

Crocodile: clerestory Sports window.

Dog: Sports window.

Donkey: Statue in north transept, St. James Chapel.

Doves: seven in Lesser Rose window; clerestory Arts window; clerestory Communications rose window; All Souls' reredos; clerestory ambulatory Seven Plagues window; St. James Chapel chancel window; St. Ambrose Chapel altar canopy.

Dragon: exterior St. Columba Chapel; Religious Life window; clerestory ambulatory Woman in the Sun; St. Ansgar Chapel west (left) window.

Eagle (usually symbolizing St. John): front door, lower right portal; Golden Book; base of pulpit; pulpit fall; Lectern; niche in Founder's Tomb; clerestory ambulatory Natural Elements; St. James Chapel altar; St. James Chapel right wall; St. Ambrose Chapel left wall; baptistry wall shield.

Blessing of the animals – Feast of St. Francis   Cathedral Archives

Elephant: front door, lower left portal.

Fish: front door, lower left portal; Creation window; Bethsaida medallion; St. Andrew medallion; baptistry wall shield.

Fox: clerestory Sports window.

Giraffe: nine in the outdoor Peace Fountain.

Horse: four in front door, lower right portal; St. Martin Chapel niche in north wall.

Lamb (sheep): Labor window (Nativity); Medical window; rosette of Crusaders' window (Lamb of God); Golden Book; Jordan medallion; clerestory ambulatory Natural Elements; St. James Chapel altar.

Lion: Creation window; Sports window; Golden Book; Jordan medallion; clerestory ambulatory Natural Elements; St. James Chapel altar. As symbol of St. Mark: front door, lower right portal; base of pulpit; St. Ambrose Chapel right wall; baptistry wall shield. As Lion of Judah or David: clerestory Crusaders'; clerestory Labor.

Owl: Education window.

Ox: Symbolizing St. Luke: front door lower right portal; St. Luke Chapel altar; clerestory Medical; base of pulpit; clerestory ambulatory Natural Elements; St. James Chapel altar; St. Ambrose Chapel right wall; baptistry wall shield. Nativity: Labor window.

Peacock: clerestory All Souls'; live and strutting on Cathedral grounds.

Pelican: Golden Book.

Phoenix: clerestory Arts; clerestory All Souls'; Golden Book.

Reindeer: skin on altar frontal, Sports Bay.

Rooster: St. Peter statue, trumeau, north tower; clerestory Missionary.

Shark: clerestory Sports.

Snake (Serpent): clerestory Sports; clerestory Education; Religious Life window; All Souls' window; Golden Book; Missionary window; St. Ambrose Chapel left window; St. Savior Chapel east window, left lancet. As part of Caduceus: Education window; All Souls' window; clerestory Medical window.

Stag: Anglican History window.

Tiger: clerestory Sports.

Toad: Medical window.

Whale: Creation window (narthex); front door, lower left portal.

Wolf: Exterior St. Columba Chapel; statue in Religious Life Bay.

G. Lynas

Bronze sculpture of wolf, by Kappy Welles – Religious Life Bay

Child plays on south lawn near outdoor pulpit

Mary Bloom

The Cathedral Close

Unlike abbeys and priories, which were often located in remote and idyllic settings, most medieval cathedrals were built where the action was. In fact, they defined the city. In England, a metropolis without a cathedral was classified as a town, regardless of population.

Because city planning was not common, some great cathedrals were squeezed into limited areas, while others gradually became surrounded by shops and residences. Where planning did take place, a protective area of grounds and support buildings, "the close" (enclosed grounds), enhanced the appearance and spirit of a great church. Salisbury's 160-acre close, a veritable village within a city, is considered the finest from the Middle Ages; and the fifty-three acres surrounding the National Cathedral in Washington, D.C., is probably the most expansive setting enjoyed by any urban church.

The close at St. John the Divine is only one-fourth as large; but it is one of the largest privately owned tracts in Manhattan. The Reverend George Wickersham II, in his vibrant presentation that has long served as the Cathedral's guidebook, suggests a walking tour of the ancillary buildings that comprise the retinue supporting the Diocese of New York and its Cathedral Church. We will follow the same route, updating the earlier work but borrowing Dr. Wickersham's zesty prose wherever possible. We will proceed counterclockwise along the driveway of the close, starting at the entrance just north of Amsterdam Avenue and 110th Street.

The Synod House

Foremost among the constellation of structures in the southern half of the close is the Synod House Ⓐ. Were it located in middle America instead of in the shadow of a great cathedral, it would be a national landmark and would merit its own guidebook.

A handsome ecclesiastical structure with a seating capacity of one thousand, this has been the meeting place of the Diocesan Convention of New York. It also houses the office of the bishops of New York. Built of West Virginia sandstone in the French Gothic style of the thirteenth century, it is the product of some of the same talent that went into the Cathedral: Cram and Ferguson, architects; grisaille windows by Connick; western portal sculpture by John Angel; three-manual pipe organ by Ernest M. Skinner.

Contributions toward the Synod House were already being received when the General Convention of the Episcopal Church selected New York as its site for the 1913 General Convention. At this point, two active and prosperous laymen, Bayard Cutting and J. P. Morgan, decided that the Synod House should be completed for that occasion and that they should split its cost between them. The Cathedral thus found itself in the unusual position of having to return previous donations!

A note for those who wonder about the health of the Episcopal Church: its General Convention today would not fit into three of these buildings!

Diocesan House

Diocesan House Ⓑ was one of the special projects of the Reverend William Reed Huntington (rector of Grace Church), who chaired the Cathedral's Fabric Committee during the crucial years from 1892 to 1909. With Dr. Huntington's gentle persuasion, this sizeable structure was created as "St. Faith's Home," a training school for deaconesses. But the rise of women has meant the decline of women's institutions. Like the mythical pelican, they nurture their offspring with their own blood. There have been no deaconesses within the Episcopal Church since 1970, when women were first admitted as deacons and later as priests.

Well before this forward step in the denomination, the Tudor structure became known as "Diocesan House." It accommodates the diocesan offices, the Cathedral archives, apartments for members of the Cathedral staff, and the Cathedral Library. The library, housed in the William Reed Huntington Room, contains nearly ten thousand volumes of theological works for clergy and laity.

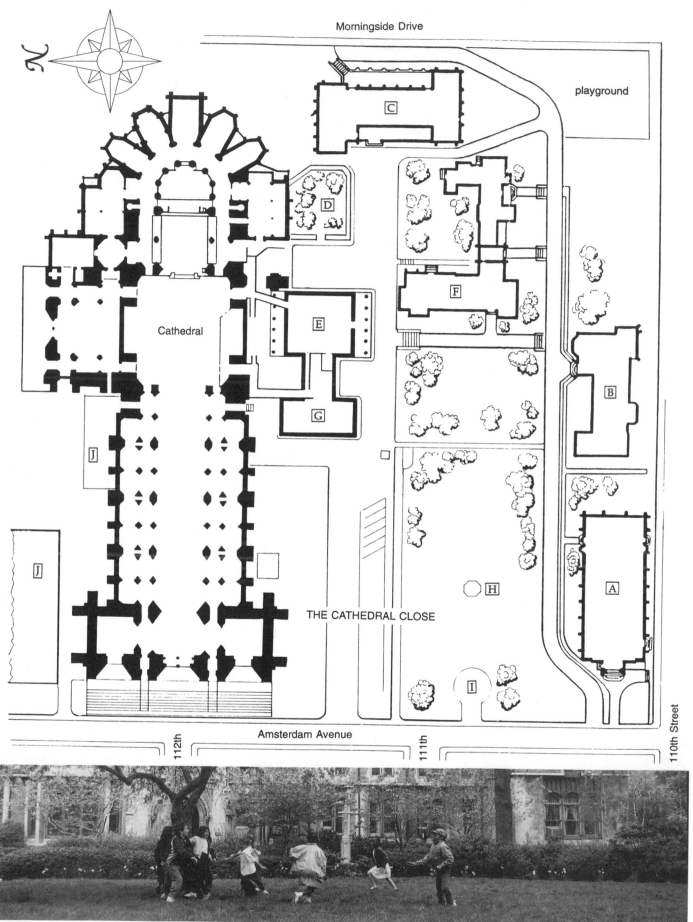

Morningside Drive

playground

C

N

Cathedral

D

E

F

G

B

J

J

THE CATHEDRAL CLOSE

H

A

I

112th

Amsterdam Avenue

111th

110th Street

Recreation on south lawn

Mary Bloom

The building was given by Archdeacon Charles C. Tiffany in memory of his wife, Julia Tiffany. Designed by Heins and LaFarge in Tudor Gothic style, it was built of Indiana limestone and completed in 1912.

The Cathedral School

Founded in 1901 by Bishop Henry Codman Potter and variously housed in the former orphanage and Cathedral crypt, the Cathedral School Ⓒ gained its permanent home in the easternmost building of the close constellation in 1913.

Designed by Cook and Welch, it is classified as English collegiate Gothic and was the gift of Mrs. J. Jarett Blodgett in memory of her father, John Herman Sherwood. The major endowment came from Frederick G. Bourne, who had served as a choir boy at Trinity Church.

In the Anglican tradition, the school started as a residential institution limited to boys (approximately forty) who sang in the Cathedral choir. Only the soprano years (fifth through eighth grades) were included. An enlightened philosophy has resulted in a coeducational day school (K-8) with 240 children, whose ethnic and religious diversity reflects the surrounding city.

The school continues to supply youthful voices to the Cathedral's renowned choir. However, the broader goal is to provide an excellent education in a spiritual ambience that honors all of the major religious traditions. The energy of the Cathedral close, rife with environmental witness, artistic nurture, and human services, is hard to quantify but easy to sense. In addition, the school's brochure happily cites "a playing field, two playgrounds, three gyms, and four peacocks."

Biblical Garden

Between the Cathedral School and the Cathedral itself is the Biblical Garden Ⓓ in which, during the course of a year, more than seventy flowers and plants of the Holy Land may be found. Those that can withstand the rigors of New York winters remain permanently in the garden; other flora are brought out only in warmer weather. A committee formed and chaired by Sarah Larkin Loening brought this garden into being. Available at the Cathedral Gift Shop is a brochure identifying each item and citing its reference in Scripture and its place in the garden.

The Deanery

Across the driveway from the Biblical Garden is the Deanery Ⓔ. Given in memory of Clinton Ogilvie by his wife, Helen Slade Ogilvie, this sizeable Gothic structure has been used by the dean or the bishop as residential quarters. It is surrounded by a splendid garden of flowers, trees, and shrubs. Cram and Ferguson were the architects of this edifice built of German micaceous schist and completed in 1912.

Cathedral House

Two years later the same architects, fabric, and style combined to build Cathedral House Ⓕ, an adjoining structure of imposing dimensions, a Gothic chateau 126 feet in length. Intended as a residence for the bishop, this four-story magnificence came under sharp criticism, which was not entirely allayed by J. P. Morgan's rarefied rationale, "Bishops should live like everyone else."

Restraint eventually prevailed. The bishop or dean occupies the upper floors. The first two floors, including the raftered library and parlor and the high-vaulted dining room, are used as Cathedral offices and meeting rooms.

Exhibit Hall

The last building in this tour of the Cathedral close was the first one to grace its precincts. Designed by Ithiel Towne and erected in the Federal style, the Exhibit Hall Ⓖ was the Leake and Watts Orphan Asylum until 1891.

As the only building on the acreage, this structure served a variety of purposes in the period immediately after the Cathedral had taken possession. All worship services were held in its main parlor for the seven years ending in January 1899, when they were moved to the crypt. In the early twentieth century the choir school inhabited the former asylum; and until 1949 the Cathedral offices and the diocesan offices were housed in the same structure. Canon Wickersham notes that frictions felt by various groups of vigorous Christians confined in a relatively small space were the stuff of Trollope's novels.

Multiple uses continue. A century after its occupancy by the Cathedral, it serves as the superintendent's office, a clothing pantry for the needy, temporary accommodations for the homeless, and a large shop for tapestry renovation.

Outdoor Pulpit

In the early twentieth century outdoor services were often held on the steps of the former orphanage. The choir school, plus men from the choir, led the music accompanied by a brass band. Worshipers would then spend the afternoon on the lawn.

Such occasions inspired the gift of an "Open Air Pulpit" Ⓗ in 1916 by Olivia Phelps Stokes in memory of her sister, Caroline Phelps Stokes. Designed by Howells and Stokes and constructed of Daytona stone, it consists of a monumental Gothic spire forty feet in height. Its use in worship was short-lived due to the growing decibels from city traffic. However, it remains as a striking focal point for the outdoor portion of the close.

Peace Fountain and west tower scaffolding

G. Lynas

Peace Fountain

Directly at the end of 111th St. stands the Peace Fountain Ⓘ, sculpted by artist in residence Greg Wyatt to commemorate the 200th anniversary of the Diocese of New York and dedicated by the Most Rev. and Rt. Hon. John Habgood, archbishop of York in 1985. Like the great Sutherland tapestry in the new Coventry Cathedral, this work of art was created to convey ancient beliefs and aspirations in a contemporary way. And like that tapestry, the sculpture must be lived with to be fully appreciated.

The stairs leading to the basin of the fountain have the form of a double-helix, symbolizing the DNA molecule, the building block of life. That same graceful double-spiral pattern continues thirty-two feet into the air, topped by the Archangel Michael, whose sword pushes Lucifer down into the basin's maelstrom. Celebration accompanies triumph as St. Michael leads nine giraffes, the animals of peace, in a dance.

The model for this masterpiece was fashioned in the Cathedral's sculpture studio beneath St. James Chapel. The bronze sections were cast in a Brooklyn foundary and reassembled on the Cathedral close to form the most monumental free-standing religious sculpture of modern times.

Forming a ring around the statue and its fountain basin is a single strand chain fence highlighted by the charming, and often fanciful, representations of animals. The sculptors of this bestiary were children from local schools (kindergarten through high school) whose creations were selected from competitions held in the 1980s. Their names, shown on nearby plaques, read like a United Nations roster.

൚

Cathedral Stoneworks

Rarely open to the public, the Cathedral Stoneworks Ⓙ is on the opposite (north) side of the cathedral building. For further information on this vital and productive part of the close see pp. 24–25.

Mary Bloom

Mary Bloom

Outreach

In medieval times the phrase *laborare est orare* (to work is to pray) gained popularity and acceptance. It could serve as the watchword for the Cathedral's programs of outreach. However, we should note that the equation is just as valid when read in the opposite direction — "to pray is to work." The work of prayer goes on regularly at St. John's, not just in high celebrations but three times every day. It is out of the work of prayer that the impulses of the Cathedral's humanitarian services grow.

Jesus established this sequence when he set forth the Great Commandments. The first is the love of God; the second (loving neighbor as self) "is like unto it."

ॐ

From the start, more than a century ago, there were clear intimations of outreach in the Cathedral's purpose, as evidenced in the threefold charter: "to be a House of Prayer for all people . . . a center of intellectual light and leadership . . . an instrument of church unity."

More recently, the Cathedral Mission Statement has set forth an outline for its multifaceted embrace of the world and all that is therein. We will use the four points of this statement (represented in italics below) as a skeleton and flesh it out with some of the specific programs that have given it life. Be reminded, however, that the evolution of human needs in a changing society requires a constant refocusing of effort. "New occasions teach new duties; time makes ancient good uncouth" (James Russell Lowell). Program lists become outdated as old projects fulfill their mission and new ones are necessitated.

1. *To serve as an international monument and symbol of unity.*

An obvious prerequisite to this goal is the completion of the great structure of the Cathedral. This is being undertaken by training a new generation of young apprentices in the ancient crafts and modern technologies of stone.

2. *To serve as a place of celebration of the sacred in life . . .*

• *. . . through artistic presentation; . . .*

The extent to which St. John's is committed to the arts, fine and performing, evokes the Age of Faith when the church was the primary sponsor of such creative work. This modern medievalism has taken shape in various programs: resident dance companies; a longstanding concert series, "Great Music in a Great Space"; a photography wall and chapel galleries featuring exhibits by young artists.

• *. . . through ecumenical and interfaith communication; . . .*

The Temple of Understanding, founded by Pope John XXIII, the Dalai Lama, Thomas Merton, Eleanor Roosevelt, Jawaharlal Nehru, Anwar el Sadat, and Albert Schweitzer, has been housed at the Cathedral for many years. It explores and expands the common ground of the world's great faiths in considering the imperatives of a planetary perspective. The Lindisfarne Association and the Gaia Institute have brought together poets, scientists, and religious leaders to discuss critical overarching issues not dealt with in single disciplines.

3. *To serve as a catalyst amid urban poverty to improve the lives of others . . .*

• *. . . through advocacy and providing models of caring service and empowerment; . . .*

Some of the Cathedral's services — the Crisis Center, the Shelter, the Clothes Closet, the Kitchen — are hands-on and in-house. To a large extent they are run by graduates of the respective programs. Others, such as Homes for the Homeless and the Urban Homesteading and Assistance Board, have spread far beyond the Cathedral close in location and serve as major training models.

• *. . . by educating and inspiring young people;*

In addition to the Cathedral school, the Manhattan Valley Youth Outreach has provided tutorial assistance to thousands of youth, offering personal and vocational guidance as well. A.C.T. (Athletics, Creativity, and Trips) has brought day camp, summer camp, and holiday activities to hundreds of neighborhood families.

4. *To serve as a center for Stewardship of the Environment.*

In addition to supporting cerebral and philosophical approaches that are developed at conferences and sponsoring an inspirational sermon series on ecological issues, the Cathedral faces ecological challenges in its own precinct with a recycling center. From the standpoint of symbolism, it is difficult to imagine a more dramatic visible statement than St. John's is contemplating with its Rene Dubos Bioshelter project, which studies use of vegetation in solar greenhouses on the four arms of the Cathedral's cruciform structure. The 1991 competition-winning design is by Santiago Calatrava of Paris, France.

cs

When we read the words of Jesus, "Every one to whom much is given, of him will much be required" (Luke 12:48), we are apt to take them as a personal, private mandate. But surely the same applies to us collectively as well. As a nation, the United States has been favored in many ways. Our periodic beneficences (the Marshall Plan and other foreign aid and disaster relief) are collective responses.

The Cathedral of St. John the Divine has been favored in sundry ways — from its lofty building site and early contributions from wealthy patricians to the surrounding range of talent that the world's most influential city has to offer, not to mention the propinquity of the United Nations. With its programs and symbols of outreach and inclusiveness, St. John's strives toward fulfillment of Christ's four-word expectation, "much will be required."

Urban Rehabilitation   Mary Bloom

Soup kitchen   Mary Bloom

Manhattan Valley Project for youth   Mary Bloom

The Cathedral Treasury

In the medieval era the physical possessions of a cathedral or abbey fell into three categories: land, fabric (the permanent portions of the structure), and treasury (the portable gifts that adorned and beautified the area and act of worship). Modern times have seen the concept of land expand upward to include air space.

The cathedral treasury can be subdivided into those gifts that are solely for esthetic purposes (such as the tapestries, icons, and other religious art, which are described elsewhere in this book) and items used in worship (crosses, verges, patens, candlesticks, ewers, chalices, basins, etc.). That latter category also includes altar vestments (frontals, fine linens, etc.) and liturgical garments (tunicles, copes, stoles, chasubles, pallia, etc.), especially when they are bejeweled or particularly ornate. The traditional title for all such raiment, "treasury investments," has taken on a rather different connotation in current times.

❧

The collective name for all precious-metalled items used for adornment or in worship is "plate." A very small portion of the total cathedral plate is shown. Particularly noteworthy is **the Kneeland Chalice** given by Miss Adele Kneeland in memory of her grandfather, Charles Kneeland. It is entirely of gold and set with many precious stones. The basic late medieval form is overlaid with a rich tracery, and the medallions are lightened by enamel work. In the canopied niches around the top of the base are figures of the Evangelists and the two great Apostles.

The Pastoral Staff of New York, borne before or carried by the bishop of New York in liturgical procession, is silver gilt and closely modeled on an outstanding fifteenth-century crozier at Corpus Christi College, Oxford, England. It was presented to Bishop Manning by the bishop of London in 1923.

Of the several crosses carried in procession, **the Cross of New York** is the most outstanding. Used only at services presided over by the bishop, it was given by the Laymen's Club of the Cathedral in memory of Bishop Manning. The cross itself (top portion) contains 200 ounces of silver and 30 ounces of gold. The staff (lower portion) contains 192 diamonds and a large oval diamond, gifts to and from the Manning family. Further enhancing the staff portion are 24 topazes, 37 aquamarines, 16 round cabochon garnets, 16 cabochon thysts, and an oval Ceylon sapphire.

Executed by Louis Glasier of New York the cross is eight feet six inches in total length and required fifteen hundred hours of skilled work by the designer, jeweler, and silversmith.

The Silver Book of the Gospels, from which the Holy Gospel is read or chanted at major liturgies and each Sunday, was given by Ellis H. and Hilda P. Carson and their children Sheila, David, and Virginia on St. John's Day 1960. The covers are of heavy beaten silver. The front cover contains a stylized Celtic cross within a basic Runic (Scandinavian) form.

Between All Souls' Chapel and the Missionary Bay is **the Shrine of the Golden Book**. Designed by Cram and Ferguson and made by the Birmingham Guild in England, the shrine, an oblong open structure of gold-plated bronze, is an elaborate work of art. The ornamentation is rife with symbolism, particularly symbolic animals (lamb of God, phoenix, pelican, eagle, and serpent). The complex design of this shrine which is more than six feet wide, three feet deep, and thirteen feet high, also protects the book within.

The book itself, in addition to listing the names of all known contributors to the building of the Cathedral, is one of the chief treasures of the church. The pages are illuminated and the covers are overlaid with gold contributed in the form of rings and watches. Other gifts — jewels and semiprecious stones — were used to ornament the front cover.

[153]

 Commentary

The Value of Scented Oil

The fact that many items in the cathedral treasury are marketable and have a high cash value presents problems. Thievery is an obvious threat. Like cathedrals the world over, St. John's has had to be more circumspect in displaying treasury items.

A deeper challenge comes with the question, "How can you hold onto these gem-spangled riches when people in your city are homeless and underfed?" The implication is that the welfare of human beings should always be more important than the possession of artifacts. One New York institution sold its copy of the Gutenberg Bible to help meet its operating and mission expenses.

A reasonable response takes form when one studies the outcome of instances where an endowment (whether financial or artistic) was liquidated in the interest of paying for immediate needs. In most cases, the agency found itself in the same straits within a few years, the only difference being that by then the endowment was gone. There is also the matter of keeping faith with a donor who would presumably have given cash if the intent had been to make a fungible donation.

A still better response is offered by this Cathedral in the number of programs and services that are carried on in behalf of disadvantaged neighbors (see "Outreach," pp. 151–152). There can be little question about the priorities at St. John the Divine. Human need receives first attention. However, there is still a respectful adherence to the words that Moses heard from God (Exod. 25) concerning the adornment of the Tabernacle. Hence, items contributed to the treasury are gratefully received in the same spirit as Jesus showed in accepting the scented oil poured on his feet by Mary Magdalene.

The Shrine of the Golden Book — A. Leonard Gustafson

A portion of the Cathedral "Plate" — Cathedral Archives

The Anglican/Episcopal Tradition

A Brief History

The Episcopal Church in America, as distinct from other branches of Christendom, has its roots in Great Britain. It is affiliated with the Church of England and other Anglican churches worldwide in an Anglican fellowship of 70 million communicants. We will briefly trace the growth of this tradition.

One of the most important figures in the development of British Christianity, Gregory the Great (540–604), never saw Shakespeare's "sceptered isle." Space does not permit listing the achievements of this devout, protean man who renounced inherited wealth, became a monk, was later made pope, and was canonized just a generation after his death. Suffice it to say, his adjective is well-deserved.

A beloved and plausible story tells of Gregory encountering some fair-haired lads in Rome one day. When asked to what people they belonged, they responded "Angles" (English). He quipped that they looked more like angels. When he learned that they came from the kingdom of Deira (now Yorkshire), he made a further pun about saving them from *Dei ira* (the wrath of God).

Whether or not that episode provided the original stimulus, Gregory gave highest priority to Christianizing Britain. When he was frustrated in his efforts to make the journey himself, he dispatched Augustine (d. 604) to Kent to establish the first English see and become the first archbishop of Canterbury (598 C.E.). He was thereafter known as Augustine of Canterbury, distinguishing him from the earlier African saint, Augustine of Hippo.

Gregory undoubtedly knew that Britain was not virgin territory for the faith. Christianity already existed in pockets, having first arrived a half millennium earlier with the Roman troops and later coming with various small groups of immigrants from the northwestern mainland. We know very little about these earliest seeds and their nurture since Britain, having no historians like Tacitus or Pliny among its citizens, remained prehistoric during those centuries.

We do know, thanks to the Venerable Bede (673–735) and whatever sources he could draw upon, that by the seventh century there were two distinct and competitive versions of Christianity in Britain.

The British/Celtic form was considered indigenous because it had come soon after the time of Christ and had survived and flourished in the far reaches of Ireland, Scotland, Wales, and Cornwall. It had its own saints, including Britain's protomartyr (Alban, third century), Ireland's patron (Patrick, fifth century), and the very popular teacher/leader Columba (521–97).

The English/Roman branch of the faith asserted its primacy by citing Augustine and his mentor, Gregory. It was attuned to the papacy and to mainland Christianity and regarded the British/Celtic version as provincial and outmoded.

The tension finally came to a head over the proper day on which to celebrate Easter. In 664 Abbess Hilda invited opposing leaders to convene at her abbey in Whitby. At that conclave the advocates of the more modern Roman form of Christianity were inspired to cite St. Peter rather than Augustine as the source of their beliefs and practices. They managed to convince the assemblage that great as St. Columba had been, the Apostle outranked him and that the continuing leadership in Rome had inherited all of the authority that Christ had given to Peter. The issue was thereby settled.

One could easily romanticize the case of the British/Celtic faction and see them as a humble, grassroots group more faithful to the spirit of the early church — a simple David being overpowered by the Goliath of Rome. However, at that stage of history it was undoubtedly better for the English church to stay in the mainstream of an ever-changing world. Furthermore, much of the Celtic tradition was preserved. Many of the provincial saints were recognized. Even today, vestiges of Celtic practices can be seen in such places as the monastery at Iona, Scotland, founded by St. Columba more than fourteen centuries ago.

From the Council at Whitby until the Reformation, British Christianity was highlighted not so much by doctrinal change or factionalism as by personalities.

• From Devon came a saintly monk, Boniface (675–754), who passed up a promising career in the church's hierarchy to become a missionary. Helped by a papal letter to Charles Martel, he evangelized with great success in Germany until his martyrdom. He is the patron saint of Germany.

• Equally saintly, though never canonized, was King Alfred (849–99), who never let power nor the heat of battle corrupt his deep religious commitment. Winston Churchill eloquently described him as "a commanding and versatile intelligence, wielding with equal force the sword of war and of justice; using in defence arms and policy; cherishing religion, learning, and art in the midst of adversity and danger; welding together a nation and seeking always across the feuds and hatred of the ages a peace which would smile on the land."

• Because Alfred's "welding" was not permanent, it was left for an outsider king, equally talented but frequently brutal, to forge a unified nation that would withstand all future assault: William I (1028–87). The Conqueror was also devout, enjoying at all times the backing of Rome. He set in motion the construction of eight of the cathedrals that still grace the land. However, some of the tactics employed in gaining victory and achieving unity were ruthless.

• Thomas Becket (1118–70), fortieth archbishop of Canterbury, may have done more for British Christianity in death than in life. He had been a key cabinet minister and close friend of King Henry II, who rewarded him with England's highest ecclesiastical position. In his new post Thomas developed an austerity of outlook and a resistance to the influence of the Crown on the Church. The friendship eroded and Henry openly lamented the appointment. Eventually four of Henry's knights, believing themselves to be doing the king's bidding, murdered the prelate in his own cathedral. Thomas was canonized in three

years and Canterbury thereafter became England's foremost shrine, attracting pilgrims from throughout the British Isles and the Continent as well. Geoffrey Chaucer (1340?–1400) immortalized in poetry the earthy as well as the spiritual aspects of these religious treks.

• John Wycliffe (1330–84) was nearing the end of a distinguished but uneventful career as an Oxford theologian when he burst on the scene as a reformer, openly criticizing the greed and corruption of England's churches and abbeys and supervising the translation of the Bible into English to reduce the laity's dependency on the clergy. This iconoclasm brought him disfavor and eventual ostracism; however, he escaped the ultimate punishment for heretics. Not so fortunate were his Czech disciple Jon Hus and the Lollards, a raucous, unlettered band of reformers who took up Wycliffe's cause. More than seventy of the latter group were publicly burned at the stake.

Although Wycliffe preceded the Reformation by a century and a half, he has been called its morning star. It is appropriate, therefore, that we move from him to that most dramatic and traumatic development in Christian history.

℃℞

The Protestant Reformation was ignited by Martin Luther of Germany in 1517 and spread to France and Switzerland before England broke with Rome. Most Anglicans would probably wish that the pivotal figure in establishing the independence of their denomination had been purer in life and motive than Henry VIII (1491–1547). The fate of his wives and his general debauchery in later years have largely obscured his earlier life when he had been a shimmering embodiment of physical, intellectual, and theological gifts. Why and how did Henry become Fidei Defensor (Royal Defender of the Faith)? Because an ecstatic Pope Leo X granted him that title as a reward for Henry's brilliant treatise, "A Defence of the Seven Sacraments," written as a rebuttal to Martin Luther. The title remains with British monarchs and still appears on the coins of the realm.

The split from Rome was touched off by Henry's frantic desire for a male heir and the pope's refusal to let him divorce Catherine of Aragon. But this was merely an excuse for an action that had become inevitable. England had been gaining increasing independence from Roman domination. The king already controlled the appointment of bishops in his land. Furthermore, the spirit of nationalism that had already buoyed Luther in Germany existed in Britain.

What differentiated England's Reformation from the earlier rebellion of Germany and Scandinavia was that its objections were political, whereas Luther, Calvin, and Zwingli had rebelled on religious grounds: justification by faith and the supremacy of Scripture over Roman tradition. The Reformation in England was in large measure constitutional, whereas elsewhere in Europe it was primarily doctrinal and liturgical. What Henry wanted and got was a church that was Catholic but not papist.

The fledgling Anglican church experienced some volatile early-course corrections due to the succession of monarchs. Edward VI, the male heir finally granted to Henry VIII, tilted sharply toward the mainland reformers. Clergy were permitted to marry; the English version of the Bible was widely used. Translation of the liturgy into English led to the Book of Common Prayer (1549), which, with later emendations, remains one of the strong bonds among the world's Anglicans.

On Edward's death his half-sister Mary, the Catholic daughter of Henry and Catherine of Aragon, assumed the throne, and there was a violent shift in the opposite direction. Romanism again prevailed and several hundred English Protestants, including Bishops Latimer, Ridley, and Cranmer, were burned alive.

However, the seed of the controversial Henry had not yet run its course. Daughter Elizabeth succeeded Mary and wisely refrained from pushing the religious pendulum back toward the left. She steered for compromise, the golden mean that has characterized the Anglican church ever since. In essence she declared that England was both Catholic and Reformed. She affirmed loyalty to the basic creed and sacraments, but also endorsed the equally primary place of Scripture in guiding Christians in the way of their Lord.

Steering a middle course was no simple task, as Western Europe had become rife with religious upheaval. On one side Puritans were pushing for greater reform; on the other, the church of Rome was solidifying its ranks and seeking to regain control of Britain. The pope excommunicated Queen Elizabeth in 1570 and urged his British followers to depose her. The unsuccessful attack of the Spanish Armada in 1588 was aimed at the same goal. In her effort to stay on middle ground between Geneva (Protestantism) and Rome (Catholicism) the queen felt it necessary to repress and punish zealots from both camps.

The seventeenth century brought a strong challenge from the Presbyterians to the north. Oliver Cromwell's influence as protector during the Commonwealth period made the Church of England an outsider in its own land. But Cromwell's death in 1658 ended that threat.

Meanwhile, a gentler challenge was forming around the person of George Fox (1624–91), founder of the Society of Friends. His statement that folks should tremble at the word of the Lord led to his followers being called Quakers. One of the most famous of them, William Penn, said of Fox, "so meek, contented, modest, easy, steady and tender, it was a pleasure to be in his company. He exercised no authority but over evil...." Those qualities have marked the Friends' movement throughout its three-and-a-half centuries. Pound for pound the Quakers, who number only two hundred thousand worldwide, may exert more humane influence than any other religious fellowship.

A much larger movement was started in the following century within the church itself by John Wesley (1703–91). An Anglican priest and don at Oxford, Wesley sought to reach the unchurched and the hardworking poor who regarded the Church of England as a bastion of power and wealth. He also preached against overindulgence with a strictness that gave birth to the term "Methodism." He could be regarded as the first of the latter-day evangelists. Wesley never sought to break from the Church of England and is still highly regarded by that communion. His image appears in several of its churches and cathedrals.

଼

Most of the early European settlers on the east coast of North America came in religious groups. St. Augustine, Florida, was established by Spanish Catholics in 1565. Jamestown, Virginia, was the first beachhead for the Anglicans (1607). To the north were groups many of which sought refuge from the Church of England: Nonconformists (Pilgrims and Puritans) in New England (1620), Quakers in Pennsylvania (1681), and Roman Catholics in Maryland (1633).

During the many decades between the early American settlements and the ratification of the Constitution with its clear separation of church and state, the Church of England was the official religion of the southern five of the thirteen states (Virginia, Maryland, North Carolina, South Carolina, and Georgia). In those states tax dollars contributed to clergy salaries.

The American Revolution was much harder on the incipient Episcopal Church than on any other denomination in the colonies. Most Nonconformists and Roman Catholics had few qualms about seeking independence; but the Episcopalians, so directly descendant from the church of the redcoats, was seriously divided. Whereas most of the signers of the Declaration of Independence were Episcopal laymen, the majority of their clergy remained loyalists. Their oath of ordination had included allegiance to the Crown. Moreover, their salaries and parish expenses were partly underwritten by the mother church in Britain. Their stance made them targets for harassment by the more rabid proponents of independence.

For a priest to travel back to England for consecration involved a long, expensive, and dangerous voyage. Even then, as Samuel Seabury (1729–96) discovered in 1783, English bishops would not consecrate anyone who refused to take an oath of loyalty to the king. The following year he was able to find three Scottish bishops who would participate in the ceremony; and upon his return to Connecticut he became the first American bishop of the rapidly forming, independent Protestant Episcopal Church in the United States. The inclusion of the word "Protestant" was deemed necessary because "Episcopal," in post-Reformation years, had come to imply Catholicism to Nonconformists.

The severing of the umbilical cord from London and Canterbury brought compensation along with its pain. At its General Convention held in Philadelphia in 1789 (just two years after the Constitutional Convention) the fledgling Protestant Episcopal Church emerged as a democratic organism with more than a passing resemblance to the structure of the new nation. Parishes are like villages, dioceses like states, the National Convention like the federal government, and the Houses of Bishops and Deputies like the two houses of Congress. The Protestant Episcopal Church in the United States (shortened to Episcopal Church in 1982) became the first of the now twenty-five independent Anglican churches organized outside of Great Britain.

These independent churches are affiliated through the Anglican Communion with an historic bond, shared creeds (Apostles' and Nicene), and episcopal structure (governed by bishops).

In addition to Bishop Samuel Seabury, other eminent leaders in the early years include:

• The Reverend William White (1748–1846), chaplain of the Continental Congress and first bishop of Pennsylvania. He was instrumental in forging a nationwide church out of the various state bodies and became its first presiding bishop.

• The Reverend Samuel Provoost (1742–1815), who was the first chaplain to the U.S. Congress and the first bishop of New York.

• The Reverend John Henry Hobart (1775–1830), third bishop of New York, who combined exceptional administrative talents with missionary zeal and strengthened the church nationally.

• The Reverend Philander Chase (1775–1852), undaunted by his unfortunate name, became a leading missionary bishop throughout the Midwest and southwest and founded Kenyon College.

Slavery and the Civil War posed severe challenges for Christian denominations in America, which had members in both the North and the South. Only the Quakers openly promoted the Abolition movement. But there was at least one courageous voice in the Episcopal ranks. Its owner was a young Lincolnesque rector in Philadelphia, Phillips Brooks (1835–93). An exceptional preacher in a denomination not noted for homiletic brilliance, Brooks combined an orthodox theology with a deep humane concern well before the social gospel had become part of Christian witness. Possibly the most popular religious leader of the late nineteenth century, he eventually became bishop of Massachusetts. His most abiding bequest to society was an exquisite poem written while he was in the Holy Land, "O Little Town of Bethlehem."

When the social gospel finally became widespread, it caused a partial shift of emphasis from traditional dogma to the personality and ethical teachings of the historical Jesus. Since it coincided with the rise of the labor movement, it put a particular strain on the Episcopal Church, which was heavily weighted with management executives in business and industry.

This time, fortunately, that church did not sidestep the challenge. Rallied by such leaders as the Reverend Washington Gladden (best-known for his hymn "O Master Let Me Walk with Thee") and Henry Codman Potter (seventh bishop of New York) it was in the vanguard of social reform.

The twentieth century has seen a continuation of this momentum through the civil rights, equal rights, environmental, and peace movements. In the ordina-

tion of women, the Episcopal Church was preceded only by the Church of Hong Kong and the Church of Canada within the Anglican Communion.

Ecumenism has become another hallmark of the denomination. It stands uniquely positioned to reach out as a fellowship that is both Catholic and Reformed. The diversity within its ranks (evangelical and catholic; high church and low church; formal and charismatic witness; traditional and inventive liturgy) reflects the diversity of the nation it serves. The Episcopal Church has a continuing opportunity to demonstrate that unity can be achieved without conformity. And this special role within the Christian fold has provided the Episcopal Church with the experience and confidence needed to give leadership to interfaith dialogues and celebrations with representatives of other religions.

Youthful participants at the Living Cathedral

Mary Bloom

About the author:

Howard E. Quirk is an ordained Congregational clergyman who spent the better part of his working life as a foundation executive. An interest in cathedrals brought him to St. John the Divine as a volunteer guide in 1981. His tours there include a "vertical tour" which explores the towers, galleries, triforium, and clerestory areas, plus a tour for the visually impaired, using Braille floor plans.

Statue of St. John the Divine, on trumeau (centerpost) watches as statues of the Portal of Paradise are carved

Robert F. Rodriguez